"The bo

Jack swallowed hard, sensing exactly how angry she was. It was radiating off her in waves. He would've been lying if he said it wasn't a turn-on. It was red-hot. Smoking. "That's me. Jack Bowden. Bowden Construction." He extended his hand, admittedly afraid she might bite it off.

She shook her head in disgust, surely not realizing what it did to him, sending wafts of her sweet perfume in his direction. "And was there a reason you lied to me when I asked to see the site supervisor?"

Jack didn't have a good answer for that. He'd only looked at Lexi, with her designer clothes, sky-high heels and flawless face, and assumed she was just going to give him trouble. That had been his life experience with women who came from money, and he knew the Alderidge family was as wealthy as they came.

* * *

Blue Collar Billionaire by Karen Booth is part of the Texas Cattleman's Club: Heir Apparent series.

Dear Reader,

I'm so excited to have another Texas Cattleman's Club book out in the world! Writing for this series is such an honor. It's had an incredibly long run with Harlequin for a reason—readers love it, and the authors do, too!

My contribution to the latest installment is *Blue Collar Billionaire*, an exciting and epic case of opposites attract. Lexi is petite, privileged and heartbroken, while Jack is a burly rags-to-riches story. She's fiery. He's a laid-back joker. Watching their personalities clash and seeing passion boil over was such a fun ride. I have to admit that I have a real soft spot for Jack. There's a lot of passion hiding under his affable exterior. He shows Lexi all she's been missing out on in life, and I thoroughly enjoyed watching their romance unfold. The common ground they find against all odds is what makes them fall so hard!

I hope you enjoy *Blue Collar Billionaire*. Drop me a line anytime at karen@karenbooth.net. I love hearing from readers!

Karen

KAREN BOOTH

BLUE COLLAR BILLIONAIRE

HARLEQUIN
DESIRE

Special thanks and acknowledgment are given to Karen Booth for her contribution to the Texas Cattleman's Club: Heir Apparent miniseries.

HARLEQUIN®
DESIRE™

Recycling programs for this product may not exist in your area.

ISBN-13: 978-1-335-23283-0

Blue Collar Billionaire

Copyright © 2021 by Harlequin Books S.A.

This edition published by arrangement with Harlequin Books S.A.

For questions and comments about the quality of this book, please contact us at CustomerService@Harlequin.com.

Harlequin Enterprises ULC
22 Adelaide St. West, 40th Floor
Toronto, Ontario M5H 4E3, Canada
www.Harlequin.com

Printed in U.S.A.

Karen Booth is a Midwestern girl transplanted in the South, raised on '80s music and repeated readings of *Forever* by Judy Blume. When she takes a break from the art of romance, she's listening to music with her college-aged kids or sweet-talking her husband into making her a cocktail. Learn more about Karen at karenbooth.net.

Books by Karen Booth

Harlequin Desire

The Sterling Wives

Once Forbidden, Twice Tempted
High Society Secrets
All He Wants for Christmas

Texas Cattleman's Club: Heir Apparent

Blue Collar Billionaire

Visit her Author Profile page at Harlequin.com, or karenbooth.net, for more titles.

You can also find Karen Booth on Facebook, along with other Harlequin Desire authors, at Facebook.com/harlequindesireauthors!

One

"Lexi, sweetheart, you don't have to do this."

Lexi Alderidge adored her father, Winston, but how she hated his instinct to shelter her. It had been one thing when she was a little girl, but she was a thirty-eight-year-old divorcée now. It was time for him to get a new hobby. "I *do* have to do this," she replied. "If I'm going to stay in Royal, I need to work. I can't sit around all day, waiting for life to come to me."

This had been a recent realization for Lexi. Recent, as in it had only dawned on her since she'd moved home to Royal, Texas, several months ago in the wake of her divorce. She'd been all too quick to fall back into old habits and under the spell of her high school sweetheart, which ended up with her getting dumped the night before they were to be married. Lexi and romance had gone off the rails. Hence, her determination to forget about men and focus on her new job as VP of marketing for Alderidge Bank, owned by her father.

Sitting behind his humongous mahogany desk, her father crossed his arms over his chest, rocking back in his well-worn leather chair. The morning April sun streamed in through the windows behind him, glinting off his salt-and-pepper hair and adding a softer edge to his sometimes-dark demeanor. "I still don't like the idea of you visiting a construction site by yourself."

"It's my job. The bank is one of the biggest sponsors of Soiree on the Bay, and I need to oversee our involvement in it. Don't you want a status update on how they're progressing on the site construction?" The food, art and wine festival was precisely the sort of social event the bank needed to be involved with. It had the potential to bring in a much younger and hipper clientele. Alderidge Bank was stuck in the past, much like her dad. And Lexi intended to shove it—and him—into the present.

"You're too pretty to spend time with construction workers." Her father was not about to let this go, nor was he capable of seeing his own impossibly narrow-minded views.

"Now you're being ridiculous." She opened her laptop bag, which was sitting on one of the chairs opposite her father's desk, and stuffed a stack of papers into it. "I'm going."

"Look at what you're wearing. A dress and heels? What if you get catcalled? I don't even want to think about what some of the workers might say."

"I've worn a dress nearly every day of my adult life. This is my look. And I promise you, I can hold my own on a construction site. Don't worry about me." *Honestly, a catcall might make me feel better about myself.*

He pounded a fist on his desk, shocking Lexi in the process. "Alexis Simone Alderidge, I will worry about you until the day I die. You're just going to have to get used to that." Her father only called her by her full name when he wanted to underscore his point. "You're in a fragile state right now."

Lexi could admit to herself that she was a bit unsteady these days, but she was trying her hardest to put that all behind her. "If I've learned anything since my marriage ended, it's that I'm not going to break."

"At least take the helicopter down to Appaloosa Island. It's a six-hour drive round trip. There's no reason for you to be behind the wheel for that long."

Lexi had looked forward to some time alone in her new car, a pearl white Jaguar F-Pace SUV. It had been a gift to herself after her divorce. It was supposed to be a symbol of a fresh start and a new beginning, but she'd stumbled since she got back, and all of it could be blamed on her weakness for the opposite sex. She'd no longer be giving in to any of that. Love, and romance, were off the menu for the foreseeable future. "Will it make you feel better if I do that?"

"Yes, actually, it will. I know you'll be able to make a quick escape."

She nearly laughed at the mental image of herself running across a construction site in heels, trying to reach the helicopter while several construction workers were in hot pursuit. If only the men of the world were that interested. "I'll take the copter to save time. I want a few hours in the office this afternoon so I can work on my list of prospective new clients. Lila Jones from the Royal Chamber of Commerce has a few ideas for me."

"I really don't want you going out into the community trying to drum up business. I have never, ever courted a customer. People come to us, not the other way around."

"We'll talk about it, okay?" Lexi stepped behind the desk and kissed her dad on top of his head. She loved him deeply, even when he could be a thorn in her side. "There might be some things that need to change around here."

She turned and headed for the door of her dad's office, but his voice stopped her dead in her tracks.

"Just remember, Lexi. There's no fault in deciding this job isn't for you. Between your alimony and your trust fund, you certainly don't need the money."

Lexi sucked in a deep breath. Yes, her finances were in good order. But she did need something other than a man to cling to. "I'll be fine. Don't worry about me." Lexi ducked out of her dad's office before he could argue with her again. She didn't go far though, stopping at the desk of her father's assistant.

"Can I help you?" Vi asked, her drawl as thick as molasses on a cold, winter day. Her spiky hair was a shock of pure silver that beautifully complemented her tan skin tone. Lexi hoped she looked that good when she was in her late fifties.

"Yes. I need to go to Appaloosa Island and my father is insisting I take the company helicopter. Can you arrange that for me?"

"Absolutely. I'll call right now. You can meet the pilot out at the pad. Is fifteen minutes okay?"

A pilot was always on call for her father. The bank's clientele was old money, and in her experience, quite impatient. "Sure thing. Thank you."

Lexi stopped at the ladies' room to neaten her hair and check her makeup. She smoothed her red tresses, fighting the frizziness that started in the spring in Texas and continued right through the fall. It was only April. She'd be attempting to tame her hair for months.

Afterward, she headed for the rooftop access of Alderidge Bank, where the small helipad was situated. Sure enough, the black-and-gold helicopter was waiting for her. She put on her sunglasses and rushed ahead, helped inside by the copilot. She sat next to the window in the small but comfortable cabin, and buckled herself in. Moments later, they were airborne, floating in midair above her hometown of Royal. Then, they headed south.

Lexi immediately became entranced by the view below. She loved her state and the varied terrain— stretches of bright green intermixed with urban outposts and dusty rural patches. When they reached the outskirts of Houston, the city that had been her home for the entirety of her marriage to Roger, her stomach soured. It only got worse when she spotted the northern edge of sprawling Memorial Park. Just south of that, over the Buffalo Bayou River, was the ultraexclusive River Oaks neighborhood where she'd lived with her ex.

Their fairy tale had lasted for fifteen years along the golf course, where they made dozens of fabulous friends and hosted countless parties. Roger spent his days at his investment firm, and the weekends hitting the links. Lexi busied herself with charity work and Pilates. But he had never wanted her to work. That should have been her first hint that

Roger was more interested in her as an ornament—
a *belonging*—rather than as a woman. The life she'd
had with her ex might seem clichéd to some, but
Lexi still loved it. Roger was the perfect guy—
handsome, well-educated, and most important, her
parents adored him. He was exactly what they had
always wanted for her—an upstanding man from
a well-known, old-money Texas family.

But that life was no more. She was all on her own
now and she needed to prove, to herself at the very
least, that she could make a life for herself. A tear
gathered in the corner of her eye at the thought. She
had so far to go. Sighing, she looked up from the
view of the city and waited several minutes until she
dared to look again at the ground below. They were
approaching Mustang Point, an elite waterside community with a large marina for yachts. When the
Soiree on the Bay festival happened, visitors would
catch a ferry from there, over to Appaloosa Island.

They were only over the clear blue of the Gulf
of Mexico for a few minutes before they were closing in on the isle. This dot of land had been owned
by the Edmond family for years. The western side
had a small resort and a handful of mansions running along the coast, but the eastern side, where she
was headed, was still largely undeveloped. Hence
the importance of construction.

The helicopter dropped down onto a large patch
of dirt, close to the bustling building site. Nearly

every worker turned to watch the landing, shielding their eyes from the midday Texas sun. Lexi hadn't really bargained on how much of a commotion she was going to make by arriving like this. She knew for a fact that her dad hadn't thought about that, either.

Lexi grabbed her purse and sunglasses and climbed out of the helicopter in as ladylike a fashion as she could. As the rotors stopped spinning and kicking up dust, she heard the sound of swinging hammers and men shouting at each other. This was an impressive operation already, with heavy machinery pushing dirt and cranes moving steel girders. In all honesty, Lexi was a bit out of her element here. She knew absolutely nothing about construction, and it suddenly occurred to her that she hadn't asked her father whom she should speak with now that she was on-site.

She considered calling her dad, but her phone had zero bars. Guess she was going to have to wing it. She straightened her skirt and decided to forge ahead, which meant approaching the man straight ahead, probably fifty or so yards away. As she got closer, her shoes teetered on the uneven and rocky surface, but no matter how unsteady she felt, she couldn't help but appreciate the view. This guy was big like a lumberjack, leaning over what looked to be a set of plans. His white T-shirt pulled tight across the defined muscles of his biceps and shoulders. Upon further examination, she noted that his taut forearms were bronzed from the sun, and his slim-fitting jeans hinted at the contours of his long legs.

Could she be so lucky that he was in charge? The person she needed to speak with? Even though she was done with men, that would still feel like a pleasant turn of events. There was no harm in looking, right?

"Excuse me," Lexi said when she was a few feet away. "Are you the site supervisor?" Was that the right term? She honestly had no idea. "Or I guess the foreman?" She hated being so far out of her depth, but she reminded herself that this was part of jumping into a new job and learning the ropes.

The man turned and straightened, nearly blocking out the sun. The full view of him knocked the breath right out of her. He was magnificent and deliciously imposing. The man stood at least a foot taller than her five-foot-two-inch frame. His face had strong lines, and he had close-cropped brown hair that made him almost look like a drill sergeant.

She was intimidated. And intrigued.

"Who wants to know?" he asked, his expression stern.

For a moment, Lexi wondered if she'd made a horrible gaffe. "Lexi Alderidge. From Alderidge Bank. We're one of the presenting sponsors of the Soiree on the Bay festival."

"Checking up on us, huh?" He stared right at her, but he was wearing aviator sunglasses, so all she saw was her own reflection.

She hadn't expected such a gruff reception. After all, she had a legitimate reason to be here. "Yes, that's right. I'm making sure we're getting the most out of our investment. It's my father's bank and he expects a report."

The man's stern expression cracked into a brilliant white smile that first caught Lexi by surprise, then made her knees go weak. "I'm sorry. I'm just giving you a hard time. It's been a tough day on-site, and we can always use a bit of levity." He swiped off his sunglasses and laughed. His whole face lit up, the most enchanting features of which were his warm brown eyes and mesmerizing dimples.

Lexi nervously tried to match his laughter, but it came out as a pathetic titter. She'd never spent much time around men like him, so deliciously rough around the edges. "Oh. Okay." She took a deep breath, doing her best to keep her cool. "So, your boss? Is he available? Or she? I suppose a woman can work construction, too, can't she?"

"Absolutely." He surveyed her up and down, his gaze lingering for a few nervous heartbeats. "Are you looking for a job?"

"No." She felt ridiculous the minute she'd answered. He wasn't taking her seriously and she didn't appreciate it. "I'm not. I'm looking for your boss."

"Lexi!" Another man's voice sounded behind her.

She turned, just as Ross Edmond, son of Royal billionaire businessman Rusty Edmond, approached. He was quite literally one of the last people she wanted to see right now, but she wasn't surprised he was there. As a member of the festival advisory board, it was understandable that he'd be on site at least some of the time. Lexi had met hundreds of guys like Ross in her life—effortlessly handsome, born with a silver spoon in his mouth and accustomed to getting exactly what he wanted. His family owned this island, and their fathers were old acquaintances.

Despite their families' familiarity, chatting with Ross was not going to be fun. Ross's mom, Sarabeth, had recently returned to Royal, fallen head over heels in love and gotten engaged. The man who put a big fat diamond on Sarabeth's finger and professed his undying devotion? Brett Harston, Lexi's first love, and the man who six short weeks ago, had left her at the altar.

Jack Bowden didn't quite know what to make of Lexi Alderidge. Sure, he knew what he'd thought on first sight, that this redhead with the bright green eyes and killer curves was one of the sexiest women to stroll into view in quite some time. She might be petite in stature, but everything about her attitude said she was a spitfire. He had a real weakness for a spirited woman.

Oh, how he loved a challenge…

Still, he was feeling a bit guilty for toying with her and not owning up to the fact that he was not only the boss on this construction site, he was the owner of Bowden Construction. He'd have to get around to sharing that once Lexi was done talking to Ross Edmond.

"How are you holding up? I'm so sorry about everything." Ross's voice dripped with pity as he spoke to Lexi. That made Jack's ears perk up, even when he was trying to focus his attention on the festival site plans. What could a woman like Lexi Alderidge possibly have in her life that would make anyone feel sorry for her?

"I'm fine. Totally fine." Her spine stiffened and she proudly stuck out her chin, but Jack saw right through it. Lexi was definitely *not* okay. She was deflecting.

"I'm sure it's hard." Ross reached out and gently patted her shoulder. "I just wish everyone back in Royal would finally let it go for your sake. But you know how it goes. Royal loves a juicy story, and you don't get much juicier than a bride and a runaway groom."

Runaway groom. Oh, crap. Jack realized then that he'd heard about Lexi; he simply hadn't made the connection between her and the bank with her family's name on it. She was the woman from Royal who'd been left at the altar. *Ouch.* He had been dumped before, and the timing had been very similar, but it had happened long ago and not in such a publicly humiliating way.

"Well, you know what it's like when everyone talks about you, right? All I've been hearing about is your fight with your dad. Please tell me that he hasn't actually disowned you." Lexi's tone was sweet, but there was no mistaking the bite behind it. It was all "bless your heart" without actually meaning the words she was saying.

Jack loved hearing her stick up for herself, but he couldn't ignore his protective urges, the way he wanted badly to intervene and put a stop to this. He had three younger sisters, after all, and he didn't know another way to react to a woman in trouble.

"My dad doesn't matter. I wouldn't trade my life with Charlotte for anything. I'm with my soul mate," Ross said, trying to play it off. "I hope the same for you, Lexi. That you can find happiness like I have. Plenty of fish in the sea, and you have a lot to offer. I'm sure you'll meet someone."

She'd been left at the altar, and Ross was reminding her that she was apparently unattached at the moment? That last part was a slice of good news for Jack, served with a side of bad for Lexi. Jack couldn't witness any more of this. He cleared his throat and hoped to hell Lexi wasn't going to react to what he was about to say by elbowing him in the groin. "Now hold on a minute."

She turned toward him, her eyes wide with bewilderment.

Jack had to keep going. He'd started this and now he was going to finish it. Resolute, he reached for her hand. Her skin was just as velvety smooth as it looked, and his fingers practically swallowed hers up. "Lexi, you'd better set the record straight with Ross, don't you think? It's early days, but we've got a pretty good thing going." As he peered down at her, wordlessly trying to explain his plan, he was tempted to dive right into her crystalline green eyes. Especially when she arched one eyebrow at him, silently telling him that he was nuts.

But then she surprised him by knocking back her head and unleashing a musical giggle. She returned her sights to Ross. "I was a little afraid to say anything since the rumor mill refuses to stop talking about me."

Ross's stare narrowed. "You and Jack? You're dating?"

Jack realized what a close call that had been. He hadn't even told Lexi his name. "Yep," Jack said. "How lucky am I?"

A skeptical smile crossed the other man's face. "That's great. I'm very happy for you."

Jack squeezed her hand a little tighter.

"Thanks," Lexi said. "That's why I came to the festival site today. Had to check up on him."

"Checking up on the boss. I like it." Ross's cell phone rang and he fished it out of his pocket. "Oh, shoot. I really need to answer this. It's one of the other festival board members. I'll talk to you two soon." He wandered off, leaving Jack and Lexi alone.

It took a fraction of a second before she yanked back her hand. "The boss? *You're* the boss?"

Jack swallowed hard, sensing exactly how angry she was. It was radiating off her in waves. He would've been lying if he said it wasn't a turn-on. "That's me. Jack Bowden. Bowden Construction." He extended his hand, admittedly afraid she might bite it off.

She shook her head in utter disgust, surely not realizing what it did to him, sending wafts of her sweet perfume in his direction. "And was there a reason you lied to me when I asked to see the site supervisor?"

Jack didn't have a good answer for that. He'd only looked at Lexi, with her designer clothes, sky-high heels and flawless face, and assumed she was going to give him trouble. That had been the totality of his life experience with women who came from money, and he knew the Alderidge family was as wealthy as they came. "I was just kidding around."

"Is it your gut instinct to give a woman a hard

time? Just because I don't look like I belong on a construction site?"

Jack felt bad now. His propensity for joking around often got him in trouble, but he'd learned long ago not to take everything so seriously. "I'm sorry. Truly, I am."

"I just don't think it's appropriate in a professional setting. I'm here to discuss business, and you're trying to play a prank on me? And then you jump in with that ludicrous story about us dating? It's *preposterous*!"

Jack took issue with that last part. "Why exactly is it, as you put it, preposterous?"

"I think that's fairly obvious."

He tried not to be too insulted, reminding himself that he was wearing jeans, a T-shirt and work boots. Lexi was obviously more accustomed to men like Ross, who didn't think twice about wearing a Rolex and eight hundred-dollar shoes to a site that was all dirt and grime. "I was trying to help you out of a jam."

"I don't recall asking for your help."

Something told him that it wasn't going to go over well if he explained that he had a real weakness for a damsel in distress. He'd save that excuse for another time. "I couldn't listen to him talk to you like that. I don't know what happened with your wedding, but I'm sure that whoever left you at the altar is a certifiable idiot. No woman deserves to be on the receiving end of that, but especially not one who's so beautiful."

Lexi's posture softened and Jack was struck by an image of her in his arms, breathless from his kiss. Logic said he should swipe it away, but he didn't want to. "I'm the dumb one. But thank you. I appreciate that."

"Can we start over?" He offered his hand, trying to shake free his illicit thoughts of Lexi and the way he couldn't stop wondering if the rest of her delectable body was as soft as her hand. "Jack Bowden. Bowden Construction."

The faintest smile crossed Lexi's luscious lips, which wasn't helping Jack focus. "Lexi Alderidge. Alderidge Bank."

"What can I help you with today, Ms. Alderidge?"

"I came to check the progress on the festival construction. I was hoping you could tell me more about it. Show me around a little bit."

Jack didn't want to ogle Lexi in a professional setting, but his vision dropped to the impractical heels she was wearing. They made her lithe legs look impossibly good. The contrast of the sleek black leather and her creamy skin was too much to take. "I'm sorry, but I can't let you walk around the site in those shoes. It's not safe. You'll hurt yourself, and if that happens, it'll be my fault. I could never forgive myself."

"Are you saying I came all this way for nothing?"

"If you'd let me know ahead of time that you were coming, I could have planned accordingly."

"You can't show me anything? I need to be able to tell my dad something when I get back to the office." There was an edge of desperation in her voice that hadn't been there a few moments ago, not even when she'd had Ross reminding her of her personal problems.

"I take it your dad is Winston Alderidge?"

"He is. You aren't one of our customers, are you?"

Jack cleared his throat and tried to not let the memory of his one run-in with the banking mogul ruin his day. "No. Definitely not."

"I didn't think so."

Jack ignored the subtle inference that a guy like him wouldn't have an account with Alderidge Bank, what with their sizable account minimums. He wasn't about to inform her that a man who owned a construction company, but who also wasn't afraid to get his hands dirty on-site for a highly important project, might have more money than he knew what to do with. "I could show you the plans. At least tell you where we are in the process."

"I guess that could be okay."

"Come on." Jack waved her over to the worktable where he kept the site plans. He got another whiff of her sweet floral scent when she stood next to him. It was heavenly, like a meadow of wildflowers at the peak of a Texas summer. "There's a lot to do before the festival. Here's where the stages are going, but we're also constructing outbuildings for the various VIP areas, facilities for food preparation, and bringing water and electricity to this side of the island. You name it."

"Wow." Lexi leaned closer to him as she surveyed the plans. She clearly had no idea of the effect she was having on him, but Jack was painfully aware as a wave of tingling warmth came over him. It hadn't been long since he'd been this close to a woman, but it had been a lifetime since he'd had one pique his interest like this. "Do you think you'll have enough time to get this all done?" She turned around and looked out over the work site. It was still largely a vast pile of dirt. "I don't know much about construction, but it seems like a very big job."

Jack had known from the beginning that they were biting off a bit more than they could chew with this festival, but with Rusty Edmond bankrolling the project, he believed they could pull it off. Money had a way of making everything easier. Having come from very little, Jack had learned that lesson many times. "We'll get it done. We're about to start rotating crews and working longer shifts."

Lexi smiled at him sweetly, delivering another pang of guilt over having given her a hard time when she'd arrived. "If I wear different shoes, can I come back to see the progress?"

Jack was hit with a glimmer of optimism at the thought of that. "Of course." He reached into his pocket and pulled out a business card. "Here's my number. Just call or text me ahead of time and I'll be sure to clear my schedule."

Lexi looked at the card. "There you are. Owner, Bowden Construction. Very impressive."

Something told him she wasn't all that impressed, but he'd take it. "You know, I'd like to apologize again for the way I acted when you first arrived. I shouldn't have done that."

"Apology accepted, Jack. It's old news at this point."

"I'd like to make it up to you if I can. Dinner? In Royal?"

"Do you live there?"

"I do. Out in the sticks." Jack skipped the part about twenty acres of land and a magnificent custom home with a massive pool. He wasn't the bragging type. And would rather *show* a woman what he was worth, not tell her about it.

"Well, sure. That would be fine."

"I mean, we *are* dating," he said with a wink. "We should probably be seen in public. At least once."

Two

Jack wasn't proud of it, but he'd looked up Lexi Alderidge online as soon as he returned home from the job site Thursday evening. It was a move made solely for self-preservation. He already knew he didn't like Lexi's dad, Winston, so he had to know what his offspring were like. He'd made a few mistakes when it came to women over the years, and he wanted to know exactly what he was getting into by taking Lexi Alderidge out on the town.

Much of what Jack found online was reporting on Lexi's recent divorce. Her now-former husband was Roger Harrington from Houston, a man of considerable means. Lexi and Roger had been married for nearly fifteen years before the split, but they hadn't had children, which was probably a good thing considering how things ended. Jack's parents were happily married, but he had plenty of friends who'd struggled with it when their parents split up.

Irreconcilable differences were cited as the reason for the divorce, but Jack had suspicions that might not be the whole story. Roger was photographed weeks later at a charity event with a much younger woman on his arm. Jack knew guys like Roger, who were born with a big bank account, attended the finest of schools and never wanted for a single thing in life. Although Jack didn't want to invest much energy into thinking about how his own life had wildly differed from that path, he did hate that the arrogant jerk had insulted Lexi by picking up so quickly with another woman. Perhaps Jack could take away some sting from that rebuke. It sure made him want to treat her like a queen.

A few minutes before seven on Friday night, he pulled up to the guarded entrance of Pine Valley, the ritzy gated golf community where Lexi had told him she lived. "Jack Bowden. Lexi Alderidge should have left my name," he said to the man working security.

"Yes, sir. Do you know where you're headed?" The guard stepped out of the small outbuilding and pointed off to the east. "The Alderidge family compound is along that end of the golf course."

"Family compound?"

"Yes, sir. Winston and Annemarie have lived here since their girls were little. Ms. Lexi is staying in their guest cottage. Once you get past their gate, keep to the right of the main house and continue until you run out of road."

For an instant, Jack considered turning around. Lexi had left out the part about living on her parents' property. He didn't relish a run-in with her father. The one he'd had several years ago had not ended well, and Jack didn't want to embarrass Lexi. Then again, it might be good for the Alderidge family to have someone like him shake up their utopia. "I'll find my way. Thank you."

As Jack drove down the winding tree-lined streets of Lexi's neighborhood, with its stately mansions and pristine lawns, he knew very well that he couldn't be any farther removed from the life he'd had before he came to Royal eleven years ago. This much money and prestige had never been part of his upbringing in San Antonio, and frankly, he preferred it that way. He took immense pride in how hard he'd worked to be driving a Bentley Bentayga SUV with a panoramic sunroof, custom leather upholstery, and some serious horsepower under the hood. The first time he'd driven into Royal, heartbroken but determined to succeed, he'd had nothing but big dreams and a rusty old Ford pickup. How times had changed.

He finally reached the Alderidge home, which in all reality looked more like a fortress. A tall ivy-covered stone wall surrounded the property, with a large wrought-iron gate. Lexi had given Jack the security code, but it didn't make him feel any better about pulling into Winston Aldcridge's driveway.

The house was still several hundred yards ahead, with a wraparound front porch and plenty of Southern charm. There were lights on inside the house, and he did wonder for a moment if Lexi's dad was the type to peer out the window to see who was driving around back to pick up his daughter. Jack didn't put too much thought into it though. He'd have his moment with Winston someday, and then he'd tell him exactly what he thought of him.

As directed, Jack pulled around the side of the main house, driving past a five-bay garage, then a lush pool area and even a putting green. Ahead, he could see the guesthouse, an elegant white cottage, complete with flower-filled window boxes, tall lead-paned windows, and an arched portico to shield the entrance from the elements. It was the upgraded version of a fairy tale, and in Jack's mind, the sort of place a princess would live. He pulled up in front and strolled to the front door, wondering for about the one hundredth time what in the world he was getting himself into. Maybe he should have just let Lexi twist in the wind when Ross had been talking to her yesterday.

But then he rang the bell, and as soon as she answered, he realized he'd done the exact right thing. She was breathtaking in a simple sleeveless red dress with a plunging neckline. It was hard to know where to look. She had so many spellbinding curves and was truly a feast for the eyes.

"Hi," Lexi said softly. "Did you find the place okay?"

"I did." He folded his hands in front of him and peeked inside, waiting for an invitation.

Lexi shook her head as if she was distracted. "I'm sorry. Why don't you come in for a minute while I grab my bag?"

Jack stepped inside and closed the door behind him. All he could think as he took in a view of the house was that the Alderidge's guests were very lucky to be able to stay in such a finely appointed place. It was decorated with elegant, but comfortable furnishings like overstuffed sofas and chairs, but everything was upholstered in bright white. Definitely not the place for dogs or children or anything messy. "Beautiful place you've got here."

"Thanks. I'm not staying. This is…temporary. It was an easy choice when I came back to Royal, but I can't live under my parents' noses forever."

"How long have you been back?"

"It's been almost five months. I was in Houston before this."

"Gotcha." Jack didn't want to let on that he knew

about her divorce. But the one thing he didn't know the details of was the part about being left at the altar. There may have been buzz around Royal, but he hadn't seen anything online. Perhaps he'd ask about it over dinner. After several glasses of wine. "Are you ready to go? I made a reservation at Sheen for seven thirty."

Lexi turned and checked her makeup in a mirror hanging on the wall. "You shouldn't feel like you have to impress me, Jack. I'm happy going any-where. We could go to the Royal Diner if you want. Great pie. Sheen is so pricy. Or we could go dutch."

Sheen was a newer restaurant in Royal, housed in a remarkable building made entirely of glass. The cuisine was top-notch, but it did indeed have the price tag to match. "That's where I want to go. I love the food. That dish the chef makes with the braised beef over Thai noodles? It's amazing."

She dropped a lipstick into her bag and cast him a look of surprise. "You've been?"

Jack would've corrected her if he wasn't so amused by the things she loved to assume. Plus, he felt that this was a bit of a test of her true colors. "Many times." He offered his arm. "Now giddyap or we'll be late."

Lexi hooked her arm in his and out the door they went, but they didn't get far before she came to a stop. "Is that your car?"

"It'd better be. It's what I drove here."

She cast him a sideways glance. "You love to joke around, don't you?"

"Guilty as charged. Were you expecting me to be driving something else?"

"No. I mean, yes. Frankly, it does surprise me. I had no idea the construction business was so lucrative."

Jack rounded to the passenger side and opened the car door for her, laughing under his breath. Any other guy would be more than insulted by Lexi's comment, but he wasn't about to let it bother him. If anything, he saw it as a challenge to show her exactly what and who he was. "Lexi, I'm the *owner* of Bowden Construction. We have millions of dollars in projects going at any one time. You'd be surprised." She climbed in and he shut the door behind her. "Apparently," he muttered under his breath as he ambled to his side of the car and climbed in.

She fastened her seat belt and planted her hands in her lap, seeming a bit uncomfortable. "I'm sorry. I wasn't trying to be rude. I didn't know."

Jack slid her a grin and started the ignition. Fake date or not, he didn't want her to have a bad time. "It's okay. I don't judge people. That's one of the first things you need to learn about me."

Lexi had to wonder how many more surprises Jack was going to spring on her tonight. First there was the suit—in fine charcoal gray wool, probably

Italian, and certainly custom tailored to accommodate his wide, muscled frame. It was a complete turnaround from the T-shirt and jeans he'd been wearing yesterday, and inexplicably, Lexi couldn't decide which look she liked better. They each held their own sexy appeal. Second was his sleek, refined choice of car. Third, she never imagined he'd opt to take her to a place as chic and sophisticated as Sheen.

Jack had upped the stakes with their fake date. All sorts of people from Royal would see them together at Sheen, including the likes of the Royal Reporters, her ex's nickname for the locals who circled around juicy pieces of gossip the way bees swarmed to honey. They'd all relished the epic way in which Lexi had been dumped. Her fall from grace had been too delicious for them to pass up. If she was lucky, being on the arm of handsome, impossible-to-miss Jack Bowden might get them to stop chattering about her or at least get them gossiping about her in a different way.

As Jack drove to the restaurant, Lexi couldn't help but notice the way his big hands handled the steering wheel. She could imagine that if they ever got into a scrape, he would protect her. No man had shielded her from much of anything, aside from perhaps her dad. Maybe that had been her problem when it came to romance—she'd never chosen the right guy.

Stop it, Lexi, she reprimanded herself. This was not a real date. She had zero business getting involved with any man, including Jack, no matter how sexy and intriguing he was. Tonight was for having a bit of fun and for shutting up the Royal rumor mill. If she never heard "left at the altar" again, it would be too soon.

"I don't want to pry, but I feel like I should ask you about something before we get to the restaurant," Jack murmured.

Lexi feared what was going to come next, but they were only five minutes or so from arriving at Sheen, so hopefully it wouldn't be too much of an ordeal. "No guarantees that I'll answer but feel free."

"I was hoping you'd tell me what exactly Ross was talking about yesterday. I didn't want to say anything where someone might overhear. Like at the restaurant. And if it's too painful to discuss, feel free to punch me in the arm or tell me to mind my own business."

Lexi couldn't help but smile, even when this was her least favorite subject of all time. Jack was more than a surprise; he was a true Texas gentleman. She'd been embarrassed more often than she could count in the last six or seven months, and here he was trying to prevent that from happening again. She greatly appreciated the gesture. It almost made her want to tell him every last painful detail. *Almost.*

"Brett Harston and I were to be married, but he dumped me right before the wedding. He was my high school sweetheart, and we got back together when I returned to Royal after I went through a divorce." Lexi looked out the window, watching the Royal scenery, wondering if she'd ever stop feeling so damn weepy when telling this story. "Brett and I were drawn together. I think it felt familiar. I convinced myself we were in love again, but we weren't. It was comfortable." She turned to look at him, admiring his strong profile. "Does that sound crazy?"

He gave her a reassuring glance. "Not at all."

It wasn't much consolation, but she'd take it. "I pressured him into the wedding. It was my fault. My father's opinion of him didn't help."

"He didn't like Brett?"

"My mother helped me plan the wedding because that was what I wanted, but my father still saw him the way he was when we first met. Not the sort of guy he wanted for his daughter." Lexi stopped there, knowing that if she explained further, she'd likely insult Jack. Her father had objected because Brett had a very modest background. "That's probably more than you ever wanted to know."

Jack shook his head. "No. I just don't like hearing you blame yourself. I realize I don't know you well, but it doesn't strike me as right." He turned into the parking lot at Sheen. The glass structure was all lit up against the dark Royal sky. Then, after pulling up to the valet stand and killing the ignition, he turned over his keys to the attendant and met Lexi on the sidewalk. Just like he had at her place, he offered his arm, but he stopped before they went inside. "I have a proposal for you, Lexi." His voice was deep and calm as he peered down at her.

She found it difficult to swallow. His eyes were so warm and comforting, and after the things he'd said in the car, she didn't quite know what to make of him. Even with her determination to stay away from men, she could imagine how nice it would be to have Jack Bowden's eyes be the last thing she saw before she went to sleep. Or the first thing she saw when she woke up. "What's that, Jack?"

"Let's not talk about any man who couldn't find a way to be good to you. Let's let tonight be all about looking ahead."

Lexi was flabbergasted. Where in the heck had this man been all her life? Maybe she needed to go on fake dates more often. This one was going perfectly. "You're full of surprises tonight, aren't you?"

He grinned and reached for the door. "The night's not over yet."

Lexi was swept inside, immediately inundated by the sights and sounds of the bustling restaurant. The place was packed, with customers dining at every table, enjoying cocktails in the bar, and a sizable line was waiting to speak with the host. Jack and Lexi took their place in the queue, and she tried to ignore the conflicting thoughts that were whirling through her. Part of her wished no one would see her, and she could enjoy her evening with Jack, getting to know more about him. Another part of her hoped *everyone* would see her and become convinced that she had rebounded from her heartache in spectacular fashion.

A willowy woman with bronze skin and thick brunette hair swept up in an elegant twist came from the back of the dining room and spoke to the host. She surveyed the line of waiting diners, then her eyes lit up when she seemed to see Lexi and Jack. She waved, and to Lexi's surprise, Jack waved back.

"I don't think we'll be waiting much longer," he muttered into her ear as the woman approached.

"Jack! I knew I saw your name on the reservation list." The woman and Jack embraced warmly, making Lexi wonder if she was an ex. "I can't believe you didn't call me directly. You know I'll always get you a table."

"Faith, I'd like you to meet Lexi Alderidge," Jack said, turning to Lexi. "Faith is the manager."

Lexi then remembered that the entire Sheen staff were women, a detail put in place by their head chef, Charlotte, Ross Edmond's fiancée.

Faith shook Lexi's hand. "It's nice to meet you. Jack and I go way back."

"Oh, really?" Lexi was sure she was right. This was an ex. Why did that bother her?

Jack laughed, and she yet again noticed his dimples. They made him a little more perfect. "We knew each other in high school. In San Antonio."

"How nice," Lexi said, mentally tucking away every bit of info about Jack she gathered.

"Let me get you two to your table," Faith said. "We're insanely busy tonight." She waved them through the throng of waiting customers and whisked them to the back of the restaurant, where she seated them at a beautiful table. "I'll have Charlotte send out something special for you. Can I get a bottle of wine or champagne started?"

Jack slid Lexi an inquisitive look, like he was sizing her up yet again, but he didn't ask a question. "I'm thinking champagne tonight, Faith. Your best bottle. Thank you."

"Absolutely." She patted him on the shoulder and turned on her heel in the opposite direction.

"You didn't have to do that," Lexi murmured as she got settled in her seat.

"We're celebrating."

She quirked a brow. "What are we celebrating?"

"Your freedom."

Lexi hadn't thought about her situation like that. She'd spent her entire life under someone's thumb, having gone from her parents to Brett in high school, then Roger in college and beyond, only to end up back with Brett. She was free now. Or she would be once she was off the family compound.

Just then, she spotted Rusty Edmond coming up behind Jack, along with Billy Holmes, the mastermind behind the Soiree on the Bay festival. Rusty's daughter Gina and stepson Asher were with them, as well. Lexi felt her spine stiffen. If she was about to get the same treatment from Rusty as she'd gotten from Ross, this nice evening was about to evaporate.

"Are you okay?" Jack asked.

"Yes. We're about to get a visit from more of the Edmond family. I'll introduce you."

Jack turned and rose out of his seat, completely blocking Lexi's view of the restaurant with his size, although she appreciated the new vista of his backside in that impeccable suit. He stepped aside and she saw him shaking hands with Rusty, the two men laughing heartily. Lexi had once again made a bad assumption. Of course, they knew each other. Rich tycoons like Rusty loved to build things. Jack must have done some work for him. Plus, they shared ties to the festival, since the older gentleman was bankrolling much of that enterprise.

Rusty caught sight of Lexi and seemed surprised, looking back and forth between her and Jack. "Ms. Alderidge. I didn't see you there. Probably because you were hidden by this big guy." Rusty slugged Jack in the arm.

Jack stood back. "Yes. Lexi and I met on Appaloosa yesterday. As you know, her family's bank is one of the sponsors."

Rusty nodded and Billy took notice of the turn in the conversation. "We're happy to have the support," Billy said to Lexi.

"Is everything coming along?" Rusty asked Jack.

"By the skin of our teeth, but yes. We'll get it done," he answered.

"Excellent," Rusty said. "I'll let you two get back to your meal."

The four of them breezed past with Rusty leading the way. Jack rejoined Lexi at the table.

"I'm sorry. I didn't realize you knew Rusty," Lexi said, still feeling bad that she'd jumped to yet another wrong conclusion about her dinner date.

"Oh, yeah. We've done dozens of projects together."

Lexi was still assembling the pieces of the puzzle that was Jack Bowden. Perhaps she'd never heard of him because she'd spent so many years in Houston, removed from the social circles of Royal. "Are you happy to be working with him again?"

"With Rusty? Sure. It's the supposed mastermind of the project I'm more worried about."

"Billy Holmes?" Lexi didn't know much about Billy, other than the fact that he and Ross were old college buddies and that he'd worked his way into Rusty Edmond's good graces with lightning speed. Rusty could be a ruthless man, and very few people made it into his inner circle. "Is it because the project is so huge and the timeline so tight?"

Jack tapped his fingers on the table. "That's definitely a concern, but I've had plenty of unreasonable schedules over the years. It's part of the game, especially when there's so much money involved."

"Then what is it?"

He shrugged. "Not sure, exactly. But I can't help but think that something's not quite right. It seems strange that he's getting closer to Rusty while Rusty and his own son are at odds."

"Families can be difficult sometimes. And maybe Billy's trying to get them to mend fences."

"You might be right," he acknowledged. "I hadn't thought about it like that."

The sommelier appeared with their champagne. She presented the bottle to Jack, who consulted the label carefully.

"Faith made a fantastic choice," he said. "I've had this many times."

"Are you a big wine drinker?" Lexi asked.

"I dabble." He cocked an eyebrow, and his devastating dimples made another appearance. With Jack around, Lexi didn't need champagne. She was already light-headed.

The sommelier poured a taste for Jack, which he knocked back. "It's perfect. Thank you."

She grinned and filled the first glass, which he took and handed to Lexi while his was being poured.

"Thank you," he said again to the woman, then raised his glass to Lexi once they were alone again. "To the future."

"To the future." She took a small sip and the bubbles tickled her nose. Lexi realized this was the first time in a very long time that she'd had any fun. "I'm glad I met you, Jack." Perhaps it was the initial buzz from the wine that made her feel bold.

"I'm glad I had the good sense to pretend you were my girlfriend."

Her face flushed and she turned her attention to the menu. She could enjoy herself this evening, but she couldn't afford to get carried away.

The meal was incredible—Jack ordered the noodle dish he said he'd been craving, and Lexi had salmon with a bourbon glaze and beautiful local veggies. As they ate, he told her about how he got into construction, about growing up in San Antonio, and about having three younger sisters. Lexi had a far better time than she ever would've imagined, laughing more than she'd ever thought possible, and feeling at ease for the first time in ages.

After their entrées, the waitress delivered Sheen's

signature dessert, a peach mirage torte with chocolate crumbles and a dollop of Chantilly cream, with two spoons. Between the champagne and watching Jack lick the sweet treat from the corner of his mouth, Lexi was definitely rethinking the concept of a fake date. She didn't need a boyfriend, but she could absolutely be up for a good-night kiss.

"Should we get out of here?" she asked.

Jack regarded her for a moment, and Lexi held her breath. It felt like he understood what she was asking and was totally on board. "Yes." He signaled for their waitress. "I'll pay the check."

The drive home was a test in patience, but she occupied herself by peppering Jack with questions. "Where do your sisters live?"

"Two are still in San Antonio. The youngest, Angie, lives in Royal now. She's going through a divorce right now, and I thought I'd give her a new start and a job."

Lexi reached over and touched his forearm. "That's so sweet." Honestly, he was one of the most thoughtful men she'd ever met.

When they arrived back at her place and Jack put his car in Park, she wasn't quite sure what to say. "Thank you for a lovely night."

He smiled and snapped his keys up in his hand. "It was a ton of fun. I'll walk you to the door."

Of course, she'd never say no. "That would be great."

With his hand at her back, he escorted her up the walk. Every step closer made Lexi's heart beat a little faster. "May I kiss you, Lexi?" he asked when they arrived.

She turned and gazed up at him in the soft light of the wrought-iron carriage lamp next to her front door. And while she positively ached to feel his lips on hers, she was also incredibly nervous about what might happen if they actually kissed. She didn't trust herself to not get involved, especially with a man as appealing as Jack. "We're still pretending this is a date, right?"

He turned away for a moment, looking out over the family compound. She'd once thought of this as home, but it was her parents' place now. The lights in her father's study were on, and Lexi knew from experience that her dad had an excellent view of her front door from there. She hoped to hell there weren't any prying eyes on them.

Jack turned back and reached for her hand. "The night started that way, but I felt like things changed over the course of the meal. Toasting with champagne. Talking about family…"

Lexi's heart seized up in her chest. He was right. She'd felt it, too. Something *had* shifted. In her case, she felt a little less vulnerable. A little braver. Her eyes drifted over his chest, her brain full of questions about what it might feel like to be in his arms. Before she knew what she was doing, her hands were on Jack's rock-hard biceps, so large that her fingers hardly went halfway around them. She scanned his handsome face, expecting shock, but a satisfied grin crossed his lips.

"I can't date anyone, Jack. I just can't do it. I'm not ready." It was her only condition. "But something tells me I'd be an idiot to turn down a kiss."

His smile broadened, and once again he flashed his dimples. Then, ever so slowly, he made his approach. He leaned down while Lexi craned her neck and raised herself up on her tiptoes, holding on to his strong arms. Time seemed to move at a snail's pace as his lips came closer and the sweet anticipation of what was to come made her heart flutter uncontrollably. His mouth met hers, soft at first, and she became putty in his hands. He seemed to sense her weakening, wrapping his arms around her and pulling her against him. Lexi wanted to take things slow but that kiss was too damn good, and she tilted her head to one side and parted her lips, teasing his tongue with hers. His mouth was warm and perfect.

Meanwhile, her inner dialogue was a race of competing thoughts. *He's amazing. He has a million muscles. I wonder what he looks like under that jacket. Stop it, Lexi. Stop it.* She had no business getting involved. She *had* to stick to her plan. At least for a little while longer...

Lexi pulled back, breathless. Her eyes wildly scanned his face.

"For not a real date, that was one hell of a kiss." His eyes had changed. They were dark and full of desire, stoking the fire inside her. He wanted her. She could have him if she wanted.

"I'm sorry. I guess I got carried away. I do that." So much for the promises she'd made to herself.

Jack reached up and tenderly brushed her cheek with the back of his hand. "I like the idea of you letting loose, Lexi. Something tells me you need to do that. Maybe get a few things out of your system."

Was he right about that, too? If so, something told her that Jack might be the perfect guy to help her straighten things out. She decided then and there to keep Jack in her orbit but take things slow. She wouldn't entertain a single thought of anything serious. "You're probably right about that. Maybe we can see each other again?"

He nodded and kissed her cheek, sending another wave of warmth through her. "Absolutely. You know how to reach me. Good night."

Lexi watched as Jack strolled down the sidewalk to his car and climbed inside. The ball was officially in her court. She might be terrified to lob it back, but something told her she'd be a fool to not find some excuse to see Jack Bowden again.

Three

Lexi woke to the sound of her doorbell ringing. She rolled over and pried one eye open to catch sight of the time. "Who in the world is at my door before seven on a Saturday?" For a split second, she wondered if it might be Jack. Her heart did a little flip just thinking about that kiss last night. The memory of it was still reverberating in her body. The man was not only an excellent kisser, he was a *different* kisser. The painful truth of Lexi's life was that she'd only kissed two men—Brett and Roger. Neither had ever taken control like that, leaving her with little doubt that she was actually worth kissing.

The bell chimed again, and she remembered

that Jack only had the temporary passcode to her family's security gate, and she never knew when it would change. Her dad insisted that only family should be given the permanent one. As Lexi's parents got older, she appreciated the security the gate provided, but she didn't like the way it made her feel like a princess locked up in a tower, or in her case, in a corner of an exclusive Texas neighborhood. But because of the passcode, it might not be Jack.

Lexi tossed back the covers and beelined for the door. She opened it and saw her sister, Bianca, staring at her phone, designer handbag looped on one arm, sucking on a bottle of green juice through a straw. Bianca was dressed for a workout, wearing dark purple leggings and a black tank that showed off her toned shoulders. Her sister was two years younger than Lexi, happily married to Kevin, a day trader, and they had two beautiful children together. In so many ways, Bianca had everything Lexi had ever wanted. Lexi did her best to not be jealous, but it still creeped in every now and then.

"Took you long enough to answer," Bianca said, breezing past Lexi into the house.

"Please. Come in," Lexi said with all the sarcasm the invitation warranted. Her sister treated the guesthouse like it was hers, even when Lexi was the occupant.

"You slept in," Bianca said with an accusatory tone.

"It's before seven on a Saturday. Don't try to make me sound lazy."

"I can only stay for a minute. I have yoga at eight, but I stopped by to see Mom and Dad, and figured I'd walk over and pester you."

Their parents were very early risers, even on the weekends. "So nice of you," Lexi retorted, plopping down in one of the armchairs in her living room.

"Dad and I just had a *very* interesting conversation." Bianca perched on the arm of the chair opposite Lexi, crossing her legs and bobbing a foot, seeming wholly satisfied with herself.

"Interesting how?"

"You went on a date and didn't even tell me? I'm more than a little insulted."

"How do you know about that?" Lexi asked.

"Dad saw you kissing some guy at your doorstep. A big guy he didn't recognize."

It came as little surprise that her parents would be nosy about this, especially her dad. Something told Lexi that they would love it if she became romantically involved with another man, only so they could have something to tell their friends, rather than making excuses about how she was still pulling her disastrous life together. The only problem was there was no way Jack was that guy. Her parents appreciated old money and the families swimming in it. She wished she could drag them into the present day, where a person's money, how long they'd had it, or where it came from was zero indicator of their character. "I really need to get my own place. I'll never be able to move on with my life with my own parents spying on me."

"Call that real estate agent I told you about."

"I will."

"And stop avoiding the subject," Bianca chastised. "Tell me about this mystery man."

Lexi's instinct was to keep Jack all to herself. She wanted him to be her delicious secret. Unfortunately, since they'd been seen together at Sheen, that was no longer an option. Also, she couldn't hide Jack from her sister, especially when the corners of her mouth quirked up into a smile when she thought about him. "It wasn't a date. At least not a real one."

"Unless you've taken to hiring male escorts, I have no idea what that means."

"Oh, stop. His name is Jack Bowden. I had to go to the Soiree on the Bay construction site Thursday afternoon, and we met." Lexi wasn't quite sure how to explain what had happened next. In many ways, it was still so inexplicable. One minute she was enduring Ross Edmond's pity-laden small talk and the next, a handsome man she'd known for mere minutes was pretending he was her boyfriend.

"I thought you had sworn off guys, completely."

"I have. Totally." Even Lexi wasn't so convinced anymore. "But Jack swooped in when Ross Edmond was asking a few too many prying questions about everything that happened with Brett. I think the minute Jack overheard the part about being left at the altar, he felt sorry for me. So, he told Ross that we were dating." Since that moment, Lexi'd had some time to think about it, and had wondered whether he'd been motivated to do it simply because he felt sorry for her. She appreciated the gesture, but she didn't want that from anyone.

"Wow. Bold move on his part. And you just went along with it?"

"What else was I supposed to do? I wanted Ross to go away, and I'll do anything to get people to stop talking about me. Especially the Royal Reporters."

"So. Tell me. What's this Jack like?" Bianca took another long sip of her juice.

Lexi had to think on that one. Jack was unlike any man she'd ever spent time with. He was formidable, but kind, seemingly an open book, but one with lots of revelations she hadn't expected. "Handsome. Funny. Full of surprises."

"Is he one of the financiers of the festival?"

Lexi shook her head. "No. He owns the construction company that was contracted for the festival. It's a little embarrassing, but when I met him, I thought he was one of the workers. He was dressed in jeans and work boots."

"Ooh. A working class guy. That's a big change for you. Is he in really good shape?" Bianca had a mischievous glint in her eye.

Lexi bit down on her lip just thinking about Jack's muscle-bound frame and what it had felt like to be swept up in his very capable arms. "Unbelievably good shape."

"Okay. I need to meet this guy. Like right away." Bianca rose from her seat and shot a pointed glance at Lexi. "Bring him to the library fundraiser Friday night."

Oh no. She had completely forgotten about the literacy event Bianca had been planning for months. It was being held at the Texas Cattleman's Club and would be a veritable who's who of Royal. "I can't go if Brett is going to be there. I've only seen him once since the wedding and that was plenty. I really can't be around him if he's going to be with Sarabeth."

"Do you honestly think I would make you come if Brett was going to be there? I purposely sent his invitation late. By the time he received it, the tickets were already sold out. He did write us a sizable check though. I call that a win-win."

Lexi felt a small measure of relief, but something else was bothering her. Would she seem desperate if she asked Jack out so soon? Then again, Lexi didn't want to go alone. Her sister would be no company at all, too busy chatting with the library's many supporters and dealing with things like the silent auction. "I don't know if that's a great idea. I'm trying to stay away from men, remember?"

Bianca cast her a dismissive look. "Lexi, sweetheart. You were making out with a construction worker on your front porch last night. I'd say you're failing at staying away from men."

"Don't you have a yoga class to get to?"

She grinned, then leaned down to kiss the top of Lexi's head. "Nice job deflecting. Let me know if you decide to bring Jack Friday night. But just for the record, I will be deeply disappointed and never forgive you if you don't."

Lexi blew out a long sigh as she watched her sister let herself out. Bianca had a real talent for backing her into a corner. She not only had to ask Jack, she had to hope he'd say yes. Because if Lexi showed up on Friday night without him, Bianca would give her a hard time about it forever.

Unfortunately, it was too early to call Jack to extend the invitation. But maybe that was a good thing—it gave her a bit of time to formulate her plan and figure out what to say. In the meantime, she threw in a load of laundry, changed into leggings and a tank top, then went for a run through Pine Valley. As her legs began to warm up and she hit her stride, she wound her way down the wide tree-lined streets, past the mansions and picture-perfect custom homes with their well-tended landscaping and manicured lawns. This idyllic neighborhood had brought her so much comfort as a kid. It was a safe place to grow up where nothing ever went wrong. She knew now how poorly it had prepared her for real life. It certainly hadn't equipped her to deal with the fallout of her divorce, everything that had happened with Brett, or her still-healing broken heart. Things did go wrong in real life. She wished she hadn't been so sheltered from it. *Time*, she told herself. All she needed was time…to figure out who she was, who she wanted to be and where she was going.

As to how a man fit into that equation, Lexi was still firmly in the camp of thinking that romance was not a good choice for her right now. But even so, Jack still had her second-guessing that. Perhaps some male companionship could be good for her, as long as there were no strings attached. She could focus on having fun and building a friendship with him, things she'd never managed to accomplish before. Now might be a good time to start.

She arrived back at the cottage an hour later and decided to try Jack a little after nine. His phone rang and rang, and Lexi paced, wondering if he was the sort of guy who might opt to not take her call. She was just about to hang up, when he finally answered.

"Lexi? This is a surprise." His voice was breathless, but warm. It did something to her, overwhelming her with a feeling that was equal parts excitement and anticipation.

"Are you okay? You sound out of breath," she said.

"I was in the pool. Doing some laps. I needed

some time to think." He cleared his throat. "About last night."

Her immediate reaction was to grin like a fool. The vision of Jack in a swimsuit had her imagination running wild. And his words had her heart doing somersaults. "What exactly about last night?"

He unleashed his hearty laugh, which sent a thrill down her spine. "Are you really going to make me say it out loud?"

Lexi loved the playful tone of his voice. She loved that they could flirt, and it could be nothing more than a bit of sexy fun. "Too embarrassing?"

"I'm not shy, Lexi. You must have figured that out by now."

"What is it then?" Deep down, she knew exactly where he was going with this, but there was still an uncertain part of her that wanted him to say it first.

"Fine. Elephant in the room. That was a pretty amazing kiss last night."

Heat rose in her like steam off the asphalt after a hot summer rain. "It was, wasn't it?"

"To be honest, I can't stop thinking about it."

Lexi gnawed on her thumbnail. She felt like she was playing with fire, but Jack was too damn tempting to pass up. "I thought about it all night too."

Jack groaned quietly over the line. "I don't want to let our chemistry go to waste by not seeing each other."

"Me neither."

"What do you say to lunch?"

"Yes," she blurted, then took a deep breath to slow herself down. She'd been worried about asking to see him in six days. And he wanted to see her *today*? She'd be stupid to say no. "I mean, a girl's gotta eat, right?"

Jack worried he was barreling for a heap of trouble by seeing Lexi again so soon. She was coming off two epic cases of a broken heart. While he was trying to keep his life uncomplicated, not make it messier. However, their kiss last night had changed the game. He'd told himself it would merely be fun, but it had been a lot more than that. Lexi had sent him a clear-cut message—she had something fiery pent up inside her—and he'd have to be a dead man to not be intrigued by that. In fact, he'd have to suppress every primal urge in his body to deny himself the chance to see what might transpire between the two of them.

Still, Lexi was not simply a woman to be seduced. There were roadblocks and hazards ahead. It wasn't that Jack wasn't equipped to deal with a woman who had problems. His youngest sister had them in spades, and he took pride in trying to make her struggle easier. But she was family. Those ties were the strongest. And in Lexi's case, they led straight to her father, who thought very little of Jack. He knew that because Winston Alderidge had told him as much. Their run-in might have happened several years ago, but he was certain that a man like Winston didn't go around changing his mind about people. Jack could deal with any insults that might be lobbed at him, but he didn't want to cause a rift in Lexi's world. She had more than enough to worry about.

Jack also hadn't counted on a call the day after their date. He'd thought it would be at least next week until he heard from her. But just as he'd surprised her last night, she'd turned the tables on him. And she was right. A girl *did* have to eat, as did he. In fact, he was starving. Just the thought of a hearty meal from the Royal Diner, capped off with a slice of pie, had his stomach rumbling loudly.

They'd opted to meet at the restaurant. He took a different car this time, his black BMW M3. Although it was sleek and sporty on the outside, it had so much headroom that it was one of the preferred sports cars of professional basketball players. Jack was a big guy and he needed the space, but he also loved the lion of an engine under the hood, and the way it took tight corners with ease. He zipped up in front of the diner just as Lexi was walking up to the door. Unable to help himself, he stole an eyeful of her as he killed the engine then climbed out.

Holy smokes.

"Jack!" Lexi spotted him, smiled and approached, carefully removing her oversize black sunglasses.

Everything about her was perfect—her lush red hair tumbled over her shoulders as the Texas sun caught the highlights. Her deep blue dress skimmed the sumptuous curve of her hips, with a low scoop neck showing off her mind-boggling décolletage, and her perfume trailed its way to his nose with that beguiling mix of flowers and summer rain.

"Hello there." He gripped her elbow and kissed her on the cheek, her skin soft and supple. "You look so pretty today."

"Do I? I just threw this on."

Jack cast her a disapproving look. "Lexi. Take the compliment."

Crinkles formed between her eyes. She didn't seem convinced. "You're right. I'm a little self-critical."

"I got that impression."

She looked beyond him to where his car was parked. "A different set of wheels today? Are you trying to impress me?"

He wasn't surprised that she would zero in on the vehicle, but part of him was still disappointed. He wasn't trying to impress her, and if he ever were, he wouldn't try to make an impact with something he owned. "What can I say? I have a weakness for things that go fast."

"Construction really does pay, doesn't it?"

"Considering that I met you through my job, I'd say that it absolutely does."

Her cheeks blushed with a bright and vibrant pink. "You're such a flirt."

Jack knew better than to lay it on so thick, but the reality was that he was drawn to her like a moth to a flame. "Just stating the obvious." He offered his arm, fighting a grin. "Shall we?"

They strolled into the cheery diner, brightly lit from the big picture windows facing the street. The hostess quickly saw them off to a comfortable booth near the back and handed them menus. "Your server will be over in a minute."

Jack was fixated on lunch, but Lexi seemed keenly attuned to everyone around them. His hot take was that she wanted to see who was there, and more importantly, what their reaction would be to seeing them together. She cared far too much about what the people in Royal thought. He wanted her to stop doing that. "What are you thinking about for lunch?" he asked.

"I usually do the Cobb salad," she answered. "You?"

"Burger, fries and a slice of pie."

"Sounds like a lot of calories."

"Sounds perfect to me."

Jack closed his menu and sat back on his side of the booth, spreading his arms across the back of the banquette. There was a part of him that wished he and Lexi could sit on the same side, but if she was worried about what people might say, their current seating arrangement was best. The bell on the diner door jingled and Jack looked up to see Lila Jones from the Royal Chamber of Commerce, along with Valencia Donovan, director of the Donovan Horse Rescue. Both were members of the Soiree on the Bay festival advisory board, but Jack had very little in the way of direct dealings with them. Rusty was paying the bills, and he ran interference most of the time.

The two women spotted Lexi and him, and waved, then beelined over to their table. Lexi turned as Valencia and Lila walked up.

"Jack Bowden," Lila said, pointing at him. "We were just talking about you." Lila was an earnest person, hardworking and rather serious, so her greeting came across more like an accusation than a warm hello.

"We were talking about the construction," Valencia quickly added, gathering her long wavy blond hair and pulling it back, then planting her hand on Lexi's shoulder. "Hello, Lexi. How are you?"

"I'm good, thanks. Lila, it's nice to see you."

"Nice to see you, too," Lila replied. "Are you two meeting about the festival?" Her big blue eyes darted back and forth between Lexi and him.

"Yes. That's exactly what we're doing," Lexi blurted.

Jack was getting whiplash from spending time with her. She calls him, readily accepts his offer of a lunch date, then covers her tracks by saying they were having a business meeting?

"If you're already on the subject, I hope you won't mind if I ask how construction is coming along," Lila said.

"It's getting there, but the schedule is incredibly tight. I predict a photo finish, but I'll do everything in my power to get it done on time and on budget. By the end of the month." Jack didn't want to paint an unnecessarily rosy picture, but he also didn't want them to question whether he could get the job done. He absolutely could.

"Oh, good. I'm glad," Lila said.

Valencia nodded, also seeming satisfied with Jack's answer. "That's good to hear. I think our biggest obstacle right now is getting the word out. I don't have a good sense of what public opinion is on the festival. That's part of why we came downtown today. We were hoping to walk around and find out more about what the average Royalite is saying about it."

"Jack can probably help you with that," Lexi offered.

Jack quirked an eyebrow at her, silently asking what in the hell that was supposed to mean. Was she saying that he was an "average" guy?

"He's so hands-on at work. He talks with all of his workers, and I'm sure the festival's been a topic of conversation." Lexi's face flushed with uncertainty.

"Well, Jack? Do you care to fill us in? Has anyone been talking about it?" Lila asked.

"The truth?" he answered.

"Of course," Lila said.

He cleared his throat and prepared his unvarnished words. "Outside the TCC, I'm not sure the festival is on anyone's radar. My guys know about it, but only because that's what's paying the bills right now."

"Do you think we should be doing more advertising?" Valencia asked.

"That could work, but if I'm being honest, I think the real problem is the advisory board. You all travel in the same circles. You need to get people outside of that insular world involved."

"We've been speaking to a documentary filmmaker named Abby Carmichael about filming the festival. That might help to build some buzz if we can talk about that," Lila said.

"That's a start, but I think it might be wise to get some free PR, too. Maybe find some social media influencers to talk up the festival. That's how you'll gain traction outside of Texas. If you've got people flying in from other parts of the country, then you change the game completely."

Lila and Valencia looked at each other, nodding eagerly. "That's great advice. I will work on that,"

Lila said, turning her attention back to Jack and Lexi. "Thank you so much for giving us your take on it, Jack."

"No problem. Anytime."

"And feel free to reach out to me," Lexi added. "As you know, I'm handling the bank's involvement in the festival. Give me a call if you ever think of any opportunities for us to get more involved."

"Sure thing," Lila said. "We'll leave you two alone and let you get back to your meeting." With that, Lila and Valencia wandered back to the hostess, who saw them to a table on the other side of the diner.

"Meeting, huh?" Jack asked. "I thought we were on a lunch date."

"I'm sorry. I just sort of panicked."

"Lexi, I need you to know something. I don't have some hidden agenda here. I like you. I enjoyed our date last night, and I'd like to see you some more. But I'm also not going to pretend to be something that I'm not. When you're surprised I own more than one car, and tell Lila Jones that I can be the voice of everyday people, it's pretty clear that you don't see me as being up to snuff. I don't need to spend time with a woman who looks at me that way."

Lexi frantically shook her head from side to side. "No. No. It's not that." She closed her eyes for a moment, drew in a deep breath and brought her shoulders nearly up to her ears. When her eyes popped back open, they were so full of vulnerability that it was an arrow straight to his heart. "I like you a lot. You're just very different from any guy I've ever been out with. That's all. And I'm afraid that certain reflexes die hard. I come from a family that's ridiculously fixated on things like money and influence and power. But I'm not like that. Really. I'm not. Still, it's hard to not notice those things when you've been spent your whole life around people who do."

"Fair enough. I just need you to make a conscious effort to tone that down a bit. Maybe find a way to relax and have fun."

She smiled sweetly. "Yes. Fun. I desperately want to do that. I'm sorry, but I will do better."

"Okay, good. Because I don't want to think that you're embarrassed to be seen with me."

"I'm not. At all."

"Okay." Jack wasn't entirely convinced. "Maybe you'll have a chance to prove that to me at some point."

"Actually..." Lexi's eyes sparkled from behind a thick fringe of dark lashes. "Do you have a tux?"

"I do. Why?"

"My sister organized a fundraiser for the children's literacy program at the TCC, and I want you to be my date for it."

Jack wanted to laugh. Being with Lexi was a roller coaster. Just a minute ago, she'd been covering her tracks and saying they were having a meeting. But now she wanted him to be her date at a fancy charity event. "When is it?"

"Next Friday. It'll give you a chance to meet my sister and my parents."

"I've already met your dad."

"You have?"

Jack didn't want to get into it now. Maybe Winston Alderidge had changed. And if not, he would deal with the fallout then. "It was a while ago."

"Oh, okay. Well, I hope you'd be willing to go with me. I think it will be fun." She extended her hand across the table.

Jack took the invitation, wrapping his fingers around hers. He wasn't sure where this was going, but he was damn curious to find out. "With you, I have no doubt it'll be a night to remember."

Four

Lexi worried her dress was too much. "I'm not going to be able to breathe at all tonight," she muttered to herself as she turned before the full-length mirror in her bedroom. It felt like the five-hundredth time she'd scrutinized what she was wearing. The gown was a strapless emerald green satin with a gravity-defying deep V neckline and a mermaid skirt that left nothing to the imagination. Her butt, hips and breasts were not merely flaunted in this dress, they were impossible to miss. "Hopefully it'll be worth it."

She could admit to herself that she looked good. But she still wasn't sure a dress this daring was the right call. She only knew that she wanted to be sexy for Jack. And she also wanted to show everyone in Royal that she had not been defeated by the things that had happened to her over the last year. But even more important, she wanted to show Jack that she was not embarrassed to be seen with him. Lexi knew she would draw attention in this dress, just as Jack did wherever they went. She was proud to have him as her date tonight.

The doorbell rang and Lexi darted for the door, but her progress was painfully slow as she learned the art of walking in her dress. Full strides required an exaggerated wag of her hips. Still, it got her where she was going. When she pulled open the door, she realized how poorly prepared she was for the sight of Jack in a tux. Wrapped up in classic black and crisp white, he was the embodiment of a dashing, elegant man. The cut of his jacket accentuated the strong lines of his shoulders and the way his trim waist narrowed. But the real showstopper was his smoldering dark eyes as they raked over her from head to toe—it was like watching a spark turn to a four-alarm fire.

"Well?" she asked. It felt as though he'd been eyeing her for a full five minutes. She had to know in words what he thought of her in the dress.

"Sorry. I'm still taking it all in. Or more specifically, *you*, all in."

Goose bumps raced over Lexi's bare shoulders

and heat spiked between her legs. Her brain flashed with a visual of Jack unzipping her dress, then exploring her naked body with his big manly hands. She wanted to return the favor, to tear off that perfect tux and drag her fingers all over every inch of him. Just thinking about it made it even harder to breathe. "I hope that's a good thing." She bit down on her lower lip, a little harder with each passing second while she waited for an answer.

"You're one of the sexiest women I have *ever* had the pleasure to see, Lexi. You need to know that."

She wasn't sure about the other women who had come before her. Ex-girlfriends? Casual dalliances? Jack hadn't spoken at all about his history. Her romantic frame of reference was painfully narrow, and she suspected that his might be the exact opposite. Looking at him now, it was impossible to come to a different conclusion. "You look so handsome in your tux. I know I'll have the hottest date in the whole place tonight."

One of Jack's devilish grins cropped up, which brought out his dimples. He took a step closer until they were nearly standing toe-to-toe, making Lexi hyperaware of the way her breaths made her breasts heave. "We should probably get out of here before I figure out how to get you out of that dress. I'm guessing that would disappoint your sister."

Lexi felt as though her heart was in her throat. She wanted Jack. There was no point in pretending otherwise. She just needed to find a way to keep things light and fun between them while still leaving room for hot sex. That was a balance she'd never achieved before, but she desperately wanted to try. "Bianca would not be happy if I missed her event."

He nodded in agreement and lightly traced the line of her jaw with the back of his hand. "We have to save some things for later, right?"

Lexi swallowed back her uncertainty about being both casual and seductive. "At the very least, you can help me with my zipper later."

"Then I'm your guy. I have very talented hands." Jack auditioned for the job by pulling Lexi closer by her hips, his fingers insistently pressing into the soft flesh of her butt.

She rose up on her toes for a kiss, soft and wet, tongues tangling. Jack was the *best* kisser. It would've been so easy to get carried away with him. But if she didn't make it to the TCC, Bianca would kill her, and she'd never live it down. "We should go, huh?"

"Yeah. I think that's for the best."

Lexi grabbed her handbag from the foyer table, as well as a cashmere wrap. The April nights in Royal could get chilly, although if Jack kept this up, she wouldn't need it at all.

It was a short drive to the Texas Cattleman's Club and they arrived just shy of seven o'clock, when the cocktail portion of the party was set to start. Jack took a spot in the parking lot and insisted on opening her door for her. He truly was the consummate gentleman. So much so that Lexi had to wonder how he was still single. His assets were considerable—wit, looks, charm. A highly successful business. And those dimples. She *couldn't* forget those. In total, she failed to see the downside of Jack. Lexi only hoped that the timing wouldn't ultimately prove to be their downfall. She wasn't ready for a relationship. But she *was* ready to explore what was under that tux.

Ahead of them sat the TCC, the rambling single-story structure of dark stone and wood that had been in Royal for more than one hundred years. The crowd funneling in through the main entrance was sizable. It seemed like all of Royal was here, which made Lexi all the happier that she'd thought to ask Bianca ahead of time about whether Brett might be in attendance.

Bianca and her husband, Kevin, were right inside the doors, greeting guests after they checked in and picked up their name tags. Bianca was absolutely gorgeous, decked out in a midnight blue gown with skinny straps and a full skirt. Kevin looked handsome in his tux, although he couldn't hold a candle to Jack as far as Lexi was concerned.

"Bianca. Kevin. I'd like you to meet Jack Bowden." Lexi watched as her sister's eyes lit up and she enthusiastically shook his hand.

"Jack. I've heard so much about you," Bianca

gushed, clearly sizing him up and appreciating what she saw. Lexi loved her sister, but she could be so transparent. "I understand you're the brains behind Bowden Construction. Or should I say brains *and* brawn?" Bianca smiled and patted his upper arm, then shot Lexi a look of pure envy.

Jack laughed. It was always his tendency to dismiss comments that marveled at his finer attributes. "I don't know about either, but it's nice to meet you both." He shook Kevin's hand and the two men exchanged pleasantries.

Lexi took the opportunity to pull Bianca aside. "Are Mom and Dad here yet?"

Her sister shook her head. "Not unless they managed to sneak by me. You know Dad. He loves to make an entrance. I'm sure they'll be some of the last to arrive." Bianca glanced past Lexi in the direction of Jack and Kevin. "Are you worried about seeing if Jack passes muster with Mom and Dad? Because he seems like a great guy, Lex. Well done."

"Don't say it like we're a thing. This is just casual. And yes, of course, I'm worried about Mom and Dad, exactly for the reason you just stated. Jack is a good guy. He doesn't deserve to meet the Alderidge family's grand inquisition."

Bianca patted Lexi on the shoulder. "You worry too much."

"Easy for you to say. You're my younger sister and you have it all figured out. Great marriage.

Two beautiful kids. You're the golden child and I'm…" Lexi had to stop herself before she spiraled down into overly negative thoughts. "I'm a work in progress."

"Trust me. We all are. Now go get a drink with your guy." Bianca glanced back at the crowd gathering in the great room. "Hey, Jack. I'd love it if you and Lexi could get the dancing going. It always takes forever for someone to have the nerve to get out there."

"Uh. Sure." Jack seemed uncertain about the assignment her sister had given him.

"We'll do our best," Lexi said, kissing her sister on the cheek. "Great job with planning this, by the way."

"Thanks, Lex. I hope you have fun tonight." Bianca, ever the kidder, elbowed her in the ribs.

Lexi hooked her arm in Jack's and they made their way over to the line at the bar. She did her best to focus on Jack, but she couldn't stop glancing at the entrance, looking for the arrival of her parents. Meanwhile, there were definitely people in this room who were looking at them. Possibly talking about them. Lexi feared that none of it was good, that she'd yet again become the subject of unpleasant gossip. Whatever confidence and determination she'd felt back at home was quickly fading.

"You okay?" Jack asked quietly. "You seem on edge."

Lexi managed a small smile as she looked up at him. Good God, he was handsome. It was her best distraction right now. "It's the dress. I can't breathe, so I'm basically just hyperventilating."

He unsubtly eyed her cleavage, one corner of his mouth twitching with a smile. "I'd say I'm sorry, but I'm not. The view is spectacular." He gently placed his hand on her elbow, dragging his fingers down the length of her forearm until he reached her palm and grasped her hand. Then he raised her fingers to his lips and kissed them tenderly. That one innocent gesture did nothing to soothe her nerves. It only amped up her desire to have him kiss the rest of her. "I'm also not sure you're being entirely truthful with me, but it's okay if you don't want to talk about it."

Lexi didn't want to ruminate over the things that were worrying her. She wanted to grab Jack's hand, race out of the building and kiss him ravenously. For a moment, she even wondered if his SUV had a generous back seat, although, if she thought people were gossiping about her now, having sex with Jack in the parking lot of the TCC would really get them talking. The bottom line was he was the only person in this crowd of hundreds who was making her feel good about herself. For the woman who was trying to move forward with her life, coming here tonight felt too much like she was moving backward.

They reached the bar and Jack ordered Lexi a

glass of champagne and a bourbon, neat, for himself. He spotted an available bar-top table, but it was very close to the center of the action, meaning it felt as though they were on display. From what she could tell, Jack seemed to be enjoying himself, waving at some people and saying hello to others. Meanwhile, Lexi took deep breaths and tried not to think about what those other guests might be thinking. Was Jack crazy to be out with a woman who'd been left at the altar mere months after a divorce? Had Lexi allowed herself to be distracted by another handsome face?

Lexi, stop. How she hated this cycle of negative thoughts that sometimes crept into her head. She had to stop caring about what other people thought of her. And that needed to start right now. Lexi downed the last of her champagne and plunked her glass on the table. "I think we should dance."

"Really?" Jack took survey of the room. "I know your sister said she wanted us to, but there's not a soul out there yet. I'm not usually the first guy on the dance floor."

"Why not? You like to have fun, don't you?"

"Well, yeah, but that's not really my idea of a good time. Especially with the DJ's music choices."

The song faded from an upbeat country song to a slower, romantic ballad, which Lexi took as further encouragement. She wanted to be in Jack's arms right now. He was the only thing making tonight enjoyable. And if she was going to stop thinking about what others thought, her best course was to focus on him. Completely. "Just one song." She tugged on his hand until he relented and followed her out to the dance floor.

"Okay. But I'm in charge." As soon as they stepped onto the parquet wood, Jack pulled her into his arms and they spun in a circle. "Is that good with you?"

Lexi felt dizzy in the most delicious way. As she looked up into his face and soaked up his self-assured expression, she couldn't have contained her smile if she'd wanted to. "I expect nothing less."

Jack wasn't much of a dancer. He could hold his own, but as a big guy, he'd always felt like all eyes were on him. Swaying back and forth in the middle of the dance floor in the great room at the Texas Cattleman's Club, this was one hell of a place to put yourself at center stage. A good chunk of people in this room had been his clients at one point, and the rest were folks he'd love to get some business from. It was in his best interest not to make a spectacle, but he and Lexi had already succeeded in that. Everyone seemed to be watching.

"Either these people all need to get a life or we've made a horrible mistake by coming out here," Jack said into Lexi's ear. He loved every instant when her soft skin touched his.

"So, it's not just me? You noticed it, too?"

"It would be hard not to," he quipped.

"Remind me to yell at my sister. This was all her idea. Why isn't anyone else dancing?"

"Maybe it's your dress. They're all mesmerized by you."

Lexi peered up at him. "Somehow, I doubt that. Maybe it's the incredibly handsome ten-foot-tall guy I'm dancing with."

Jack laughed and pulled her a little closer. The silky fabric of her dress was smooth against his skin, but it was nothing compared to the tender warmth of her hand. She felt so right pressed up against him. He had no idea what they were doing or where this was going, but he only knew that at that moment, he didn't want to be anywhere else but with her. "I'm only six-two."

"Hey. Don't say only. You're a full foot taller than me."

"Are you seriously only five foot two?" Their height difference was the perfect illustration of how opposites sometimes really did attract. Jack loved that they were mismatched in so many ways but were still so drawn to each other.

"Yes. I have to wear four-inch heels just to be average."

"Trust me, Lexi. You're not even close to being average." He meant it. She was extraordinary, and he hated that she didn't seem to know that. The song began to fade and segued into a faster tune. Jack was eager to exit the dance floor. Because as much he loved having her in his arms, he wanted to be somewhere out of the public eye. "Another drink? It looks like we managed to convince a few other couples to come out here."

"Sounds great."

He and Lexi walked off the dance floor, hand in hand. Just as they were about to reach the carpeted perimeter of the room, Winston Alderidge stepped into view, along with a woman Jack could only assume was Lexi's mother. She was of a similar height as her daughter, with the same red hair. Lexi reacted first, her hand dropping from Jack's. She stepped right between him and her parents, almost like she was trying to block him from view, which was not only an absurd idea, it made things awkward from the start.

"Dad. Mom. You're finally here," Lexi said.

Winston embraced his daughter, but he'd narrowed his sights on Jack. "Yes. We are. Are you going to introduce us to your companion?"

Jack tensed up the minute Winston opened his mouth. Memories of their run-in years ago barged into his mind. He had a hard time imagining he would ever like this man, however fond he was of his daughter.

Lexi's mother smiled weakly. She seemed as uncomfortable as Jack felt. "Perhaps we should go talk over in the corner. Your dad and I have a private table."

Lexi cast an anxious glance in Jack's direction then scurried off behind her parents. He hadn't actually been invited to join them, but he presumed that was the plan, so he followed. When he arrived at their table, Winston turned and thrust his hand at Jack.

"I'm Winston Alderidge, Alexis's father. This is my wife, Annemarie."

Jack could admit there was an amusing edge to this awkward scenario. Mr. Alderidge needed no introduction, and he had hoped he hadn't needed one either. "Jack Bowden. We've met, sir. Three years ago." He made sure to return an especially strong handshake.

"Jack is the owner of Bowden Construction," Lexi interjected. "We met last week when I went to Appaloosa Island."

"Bowden Construction. Hmm. I've never heard of it." Winston shrugged. "So many start-ups in these parts. It's hard for me to keep up."

Jack wanted to be nothing less than polite and cordial during this interaction, but the truth was that Lexi's father was so condescending it made it incredibly difficult. "Not a start-up, sir. We've been in business for eleven years. We're the sole contractor for the Soiree on the Bay festival."

"Ah. I guess it's good to know Rusty Edmond is supporting the little guys."

Jack was intent on keeping his cool, but Winston was grating every last nerve. "You don't remember meeting me, do you?"

Lexi's dad frowned. "I don't. But I meet a lot of people. It's impossible to remember them all."

Jack was *this* close to telling Winston that he was a pompous ass. But he decided it would be better to illustrate it and let everyone else reach their own conclusion, rather than say it right out loud. "You don't remember everyone you personally turn down for a significant business loan? Even when you met with them in your office?"

Winston reared his head back. "Is that how we met?"

"It is. I came in for a multimillion-dollar loan to expand my business. Even though I had the personal assets to guarantee it, you said I was too big a risk. Told me you would rather lend to someone who was better established in the community."

A hesitant smile crossed Winston's face as his memory seemed to kick into gear. "Ahh. Now I remember you. Things got a bit heated between us, didn't they?"

Jack nodded in affirmation. He might have said a few choice words that day, but he'd been justifiably angry. "They did. I'm an extremely hard worker, Mr. Alderidge. I have considerable assets and have built them with my own two hands. I wasn't asking for charity or a favor that day. On paper, there was no reason to deny the loan. But I have a feeling I know why you did." Jack took a step closer, doing everything he could to tamp down his temper. The problem was that every minute facing Winston made the memory of that day all the more acute.

He had left Alderidge Bank feeling humiliated and insulted.

"You took one look at me and decided there wasn't anything in it for you, aside from some interest. I didn't come from your social circles. I wasn't acquainted with your cigar-smoking buddies. I was the man who wasn't afraid to get his hands dirty. You didn't see the point, did you?"

"Well, I…" Winston's voice trailed off. "I can't grant a loan to someone I hardly know. That's not how I do business."

"You don't need to tell me how business is done. Your competitor across town greeted me with open arms. I now run my entire business through them. Millions of dollars every month, flowing like water." Jack looked at Lexi. All color had drained from her face and her eyes were like saucers. He reached for her hand, but he wasn't sure she would take it. Part of him feared she would stay with her parents and tell him to shove off. If that was the case, he'd have to live with the disappointment, but it was going to sting. "Lexi, I'd like to go. You're welcome to join me or stay. It's your choice."

She looked back and forth between Jack and her mom and dad. The wait for her answer felt like it stretched on for an eternity. "No. I'm coming with you." She slid her hand into Jack's and gave it a gentle squeeze, then turned to her parents. "Please let Bianca know I left."

Jack wasn't about to wait for more. He marched to the great room doors, Lexi in his wake. She caught up to him and took his hand again. It brought him more comfort than he cared to admit. "Jack. Stop," she said when they'd reached the hall just outside the room. Luckily, they were mostly alone—only a few stray guests were out there. "I'm so sorry. I had no idea that was the reason you knew my dad. Why didn't you tell me?"

He scanned her face, which was full of sincerity. That made him feel bad, even when his blood was right on the edge of a rolling boil. He prided himself on being the guy who stayed calm and even, but that was no longer possible. "You shouldn't have to answer for the things your father has said or done."

"You're right… I shouldn't. But I also deserve the chance to make things right, don't I? I understand everything you *didn't* say back there. I know how my dad is, how he looks down on people and makes assumptions. I hate it. He did it to Brett all the time."

Someone stepped out of the great room and Jack caught a glimpse of the crowd of people inside, wearing tuxedos and gowns. Would he ever truly fit in here? Did he actually want to? Jack was proud of his roots *and* the success he'd worked so hard for. And he didn't need invitations to garden parties and country club golf tournaments as validation. "I don't want to be a prop, Lexi. I don't want to be the blue-collar guy you parade around as a novelty. That's not me."

She grasped both of his arms, adorably craning her neck to look him in the eye. "You're not a prop, Jack. I like you. A lot."

He froze for a moment as her words sank in. He'd told himself he wouldn't get in deep with Lexi, and here she was, confessing her feelings. The trouble was that he had the exact same feelings. Even when he'd said he wouldn't go there…that he wouldn't get involved. "I like you, too, Lexi."

"Can we go talk in the car? Where we can have some privacy?"

"Yes. Good idea." Jack was sick of being here. He just wanted to be alone with her.

Lexi didn't waste any time when they got back to his car. "Do you remember that moment out in front of Sheen, when you said that you didn't want to talk about any man who didn't have the sense to treat me well? I don't think you know how much that meant to me. To have my feelings validated like that."

"It wasn't some big act of heroism, Lexi. I was being a decent guy. You should expect everyone to treat you that way."

"But they don't. My parents blame me for my divorce. I know they do." She looked down at her lap, seeming ashamed. How he hated seeing that look on her face. "They don't actually say it. They tell me that it's all for the best, but I know they don't really believe that. Deep down, they think I didn't try hard enough to be a good wife. That I should have done more to make Roger want to hold on to me. And maybe those things are true, but I also feel like if you love someone, you should want to be with them. And if you don't, then it's time to let them go."

Everything Lexi was saying was a big part of what he liked about her so much. She had a huge heart, but it seemed as though she'd been taught not to trust it. Jack liked seeing her work these things out for herself. He liked seeing her come into her own.

His phone rang. He didn't want to answer it, but there was too much going on with the Soiree on the Bay construction for him to ignore it. "Dammit. It's Rich, my business partner. I need to see what he needs."

"Yes. Of course."

Jack accepted the call. "What's up?"

"We're short a foreman out on Appaloosa for the night shift. Larry's wife went into labor," Rich said. "I know you're at a function, but is there any way you can come out here? There are a whole lot of guys standing around right now, and I can't do it all on my own."

Jack looked at Lexi. He didn't want to end their night, but duty was calling, and perhaps this was for the best. "Send the helicopter for me, okay?"

"Your house?"

Jack's property on the outskirts of Royal was over twenty acres, most of it nothing but open ranch land. "Yes. I'll be there in forty-five minutes."

"Got it."

He ended the call and placed his phone in the cupholder. "Lexi, I'm sorry, but I have to go back to Appaloosa. There are problems. And maybe tonight didn't quite turn into what either of us were hoping for."

Lexi nodded slowly. "Of course. Whatever you need to do."

Jack wasn't sure of much, but he was sure of one thing as he peered down into her flawless face— he couldn't deny how much he wanted her. But he felt like Royal, her family and his crazy schedule were smothering them. There were too many prying eyes, too many outside forces getting in the way.

"Come away with me."

"What? When?" Her voice was full of surprise, but the look on her face was one of utter delight.

He reached for her hand, then leaned down to place a soft kiss on her cheek. It took every bit of self-control he had to not take it further, to pick up where they'd left things at her house. "I like you, Lexi, but I feel like everything and everyone in Royal is sabotaging us. Let's go away for a night next weekend. I have a function I have to attend in Houston. I'm being recognized by the children's hospital foundation for an expansion I did for them last year. The Soiree on the Bay project is going to be hell for the next few weeks, but I've had this event on the books for months." He smiled down at her. "I promise I'll make it fun. I think you need to be able to let your hair down. And I know I could use a chance to breathe."

"Houston is where I lived for years. I'm bound to run into someone I know. I'm not sure it'll be much of an escape for me."

He hadn't thought that part through, but he was determined to make this work. "I already have a suite booked at the new hotel downtown. We'll go to my event, but we won't stay long. We can get to know each other on a whole new level." He drifted closer to her and kissed her cheek again, then he brushed his lips across her ear and finally, her graceful neck. Jack closed his eyes, praying for strength as her sweet smell filled his lungs. He wanted to make love to her right here and now. But she was upset, so was he, and work was calling. The time wasn't right.

"I would love to go away with you. I want you, Jack."

He grinned. The unhappiness of the earlier exchange with her dad was quickly fading. He and Lexi didn't need the rest of the world to get in the way of what was growing between them. They only needed time. Alone. "Good. Because I want you, too." He cleared his throat, distracted by her sweet smell and the display of her luscious cleavage before him. He didn't like to wait, but he would for her. "So you'll accompany me next weekend?"

"Yes." She nodded eagerly. "A million times yes."

"Perfect." He pressed the ignition button and the engine roared to life.

"What do I wear for this event?"

"You could wear that dress again if you want. You look unbelievable in it. Every guy in the place will be insanely jealous."

"Jack, you're hilarious. I'm not wearing the same dress."

"Why not?"

"My wardrobe is one of the few things I've done right with my life. I have just the thing, waiting for exactly an event like this. It still has the tags on it."

He pulled out of the parking lot, leaving the TCC behind. "What does it look like?"

Lexi drew a finger up the length of his forearm. "It's red. Silk crepe to make it cling in all the right places. And it's so low cut, I can't really wear a bra."

Jack felt a noticeable tightening in his pants. Waiting an entire week to be with her was going to be sheer torture. But he had a feeling the reward was going to be so worth it. "I can't wait to see you in it." He glanced over at her. "And then I look forward to seeing you out of it."

Five

Jack was set to pick up Lexi for the trip to Houston in two hours, and he was nervous. So much so that he wasn't doing a great job staying focused on work, which was a real problem because he, Rich and Jack's sister Angie were having their first in-person meeting in weeks. The Soiree on the Bay schedule was so crazy, they rarely had the time to sit down and hash things out.

If anyone would sense his distracted state, it was these two. Rich had been Jack's best friend since fifth grade. He'd taken a real chance on Jack by agreeing to move to Royal with him to start Bowden Construction eleven years ago. Jack had needed a fresh start in a new city after his fiancée, Marcella, had dumped him, and he'd been smart enough to know that he couldn't get a new business off the ground on his own. Thankfully, that chance had more than paid off for both Rich and Jack.

"Let's take a look at the numbers for the Soiree project." Rich hit a few keys on his laptop, and the master spreadsheet was projected on the screen at one end of the small conference room.

"We're showing a slight overage right now of about two percent," Angie said. She'd only been working for Jack for a few months, ever since he brought her to Royal after she separated from her husband, who had a volatile temper. Jack had wanted to give his sister that same fresh start he'd given himself, but he also needed to keep her safe. Angie hadn't wanted to come to Royal. *Too many rich people*, she'd said. *They make me uncomfortable. I feel like they're all looking down on me.*

Jack had swiftly reminded her that he was quite wealthy now, with a sprawling home and a fast-growing business, and that people with money were just like anyone else—some were wonderful and others were not. Luckily, Angie had acquiesced to the move to Royal, and since then, she'd not only learned the ropes of managing construction, she was a whiz with the figures.

"Do you think we'll be able to hit our numbers?" Rich asked.

"If we do, it's going to be super close," Angie said. "The cost of moving supplies over to the island has been much higher than the budget allowed. That's the big reason for the difference. Jack, it might be a good idea for you to have a conversation with Rusty Edmond and let him know."

Jack heard his name. He just hadn't heard the other words that had come before or after it. Or they'd gone in one ear and out the other. "I'm sorry. Can you repeat that?"

"Angie said you need to talk to Rusty about the overage," Rich said.

"Oh, right." Jack scribbled a note to himself. "I'll call him on the way to Houston."

"No, you won't," Angie said. "You're going to be with Lexi Alderidge, and you won't be able to focus on anything. Just like in this meeting."

"What's that supposed to mean?"

"It means you've lost your mind for this woman, Jack. And I don't like it." She sat back in her chair and crossed her arms over her chest, shooting him a piercing glare. Angie had never been one for beating around the bush. She had zero filter. "We all know where this is going. It's not only going too fast, it's going to a very scary place."

Rich closed his laptop, which made the spreadsheet disappear from the wall. "Wow, Ang. You're going to bring this up now? I thought we agreed that we wouldn't say anything until after he got back from Houston."

"Hold on a minute," Jack said. "You two have talked about this?"

"Well, yeah," Angie answered with a shrug, as if it was completely obvious that they would discuss Jack's personal life behind his back. "When a guy who once got dumped by his fiancée two weeks before his wedding gets involved with a woman who apparently doesn't know how to do anything *but* get married, it makes me worry."

Jack drew a deep breath through his nose. "My situation with Marcella was a long time ago. It's water under the bridge. I'm fine."

"You haven't had a single serious girlfriend since then," Rich said. "That doesn't seem to me like you've gotten over it."

"I've been busy." He couldn't help but notice the defensiveness in his own voice. "Getting Bowden Construction to where it is has been a monumental task. I haven't had time to get serious."

"And now you *do* have time?" Angie asked. "Your number one complaint since I moved here is that the Soiree on the Bay project is the biggest one you've ever taken on, and that the timeline is impossible. So that argument doesn't really add up. You're barely sleeping, Jack. So I don't see how you have time to date right now."

Angie and Rich had made a few halfway decent

points, but that didn't stop Jack from wanting to fight back. "Lexi and I are having fun. Am I not entitled to that? This isn't serious. It's a casual thing."

Angie rolled her eyes, which Jack did not appreciate. "I've heard the things people say about Lexi around town," she said.

"You can stop right there. I don't care about gossip."

"This isn't that. Her sister Bianca goes to the same yoga studio I go to. From everything she said, her sister hasn't been single since she was seventeen, and every guy she's been with she either married or tried to marry. That doesn't seem like the track record of someone who is capable of keeping things casual."

Jack didn't want to listen to any more of this nonsense. "You're being ridiculous. Both of you. Lexi and I are not getting married. We hardly know each other." He got up from the table. "Plus, her dad doesn't like me, and I'm guessing her mom doesn't either after what happened at the TCC last week, so it doesn't even matter. It's a nonstarter. I'm not about to get serious with a woman whose family doesn't approve of me. You both know that's way too important to me."

Rich nodded. "I get it. Lexi's dad is a real piece of work, Jack. But I also don't think it's smart to get even with him by whisking his daughter away. He's a powerful man and people in this town talk like crazy. I really think you should rethink this whole idea."

Jack couldn't believe what he was hearing. He wasn't trying to get even with Winston Alderidge. Or *was* he? Was that part of what made things so hot with Lexi? The fact that her dad so clearly looked down on him? Was this so forbidden that it made him want her that much more? "All of these points would have been more helpful to me after my first date with her, you two."

Rich and Angie exchanged plaintive looks. "We know. We just weren't sure how to bring it up with you," Angie said. "You've been busy and stressed. We aren't trying to make your life more difficult, Jack. But we're worried about you. And frankly, we're a little worried about Lexi, too. I mean, I don't know her at all, but it can't be good for her to get involved with another guy right now, especially one who her father doesn't like"

Jack felt like he had no choice but to engage in the self-reflection he'd been avoiding, but he couldn't call Lexi and cancel their getaway. She'd be disappointed, and quite frankly, so would he. He'd been looking forward to getting lost in a beautiful woman for at least one night.

"Look," he said to Rich and his sister. "I love you both. But you need to back off and let me do my thing. Lexi and I are both consenting adults.

We want to get away for a night and have some fun. That's all."

Angie and Rich looked at each other, seeming to have a silent conversation, all of which suggested that they thought he was being foolish. "Suit yourself," Angie said. "I'll be here to help you pick up the pieces when it all falls apart."

"Trust me. I'm not going to get hurt," Jack retorted on his way out the door. "I don't want serious and neither does she."

He stalked down the hall to his office to check his email while trying to shake off the sour mood he was in after his conversation with Rich and Angie. Was this really that bad of an idea? It was one night.

What could possibly happen?

Lexi wasn't so worried about her dress this time. Now that she had a better sense of what Jack liked, she was certain the red one she'd told him about hit the mark. Unlike the green gown she'd worn to the event at the TCC, she could breathe in this one, and that was a very good thing. Oxygen made it easier to manage the anticipation for what was ahead…a romantic evening at a five-star hotel, dinner and perhaps dancing, followed by their escape to his luxury suite. They could finally be truly alone, and she couldn't wait. She wanted Jack so badly it burned inside her, just as hot and crimson as the gown she wore.

Jack had asked Lexi to meet him at the airstrip outside of town, as they would be taking a helicopter to Houston. With his crazy work schedule, it was the best way to get away for a night and not spend too much time traveling. Her suitcase was in the back of her car, packed full of cute outfits, heels, a bathing suit, probably too many toiletries, and a few choice pieces of very expensive lingerie. Lexi liked having options, even if she knew she wouldn't come close to using everything she'd brought along.

Outside, the charming Royal countryside rolled by, a reminder of her lifelong ties to this place. She loved being back here, despite the recent trouble with her dad. The state of their relationship was a bit of a gray cloud hanging over her getaway with Jack—Lexi and her father were barely speaking after the dustup at the TCC. She knew a big talk was coming, but she'd wanted them both to cool off first.

Lexi's phone rang. It was Bianca. "What's up?" Lexi answered. "I'm almost at the airstrip, so I only have a few minutes."

"You can't go to Houston, Lex."

"What? Why? You said you thought it was a good idea for Jack and me to go away. You told me to go have fun. Why are you telling me this now?" Lexi didn't want to be so annoyed, but her sister's timing was wretched.

"I came across a news story about this charity

event you're going to. Do you know who's hosting it? Savannah Lee."

Her stomach knotted so tight she thought she might get sick. Savannah was the woman who Lexi's ex-husband Roger had started dating soon after she left Houston. "Do you think he will be there?"

"Even if he's not, and I'm guessing he will, you won't be able to get away from the bigger story here. Savannah and Roger just got engaged."

Ahead, Lexi saw the gated entrance for the airstrip. Jack was likely waiting for her on the other side of that fence. What was she supposed to do? Cancel on Jack? Or don't tell him and deal with seeing her ex and his new fiancée?

"Lexi? Are you still there?" Bianca asked.

"I am."

"Are you okay?"

Lexi sucked in a deep breath. "I guess." She pulled up to the electronic keypad, rolled down her window and punched in the code Jack had given her. "I don't know what to do." Straight ahead, Jack was standing next to his car, typing something on his phone. He was sporting sunglasses, wearing another of his perfect-fitting suits, looking as devastatingly handsome as ever. She'd so looked forward to this and now it felt like the universe was trying to send her a signal that this was a bad idea. "Bianca, I need to go. I'm here."

"I'm so sorry. I didn't want to ruin your weekend. But I also couldn't let you walk into that event with no idea of what's going on."

"Thank you. I appreciate it."

"Love you, Lex."

"Love you, too." She hung up the phone just as she was pulling into the space next to Jack's.

A few seconds later, he was opening the driver's side door. "Hello, beautiful." Jack smiled down at her, offering his hand to help her out of the car. "I can't wait to see you in that dress."

She climbed out, her leg naturally slipping out of her gown's high slit. That should have been a very sexy moment, a precursor to their night ahead, but Lexi was feeling like far less than a seductress right now. "Hi." That was all she could manage before she was drifting into the safety of Jack's arms, resting her head against his chest.

"What's wrong?"

"Am I that transparent?" she asked.

"You're shaking like a leaf."

"I am?" Lexi hadn't noticed, but now that he mentioned it, she realized her shoulders were quivering.

"Yes. Talk to me. Is it something with your dad?"

If only Lexi could be so lucky. She had a tiny shred of control when it came to him. "Bianca just called me. Turns out my ex-husband got engaged and his new fiancée is hosting your event tonight."

Jack blew out a big breath and pushed his sunglasses up on top of his head. He scanned her face like he was looking for answers, but she felt like she had absolutely none. "Okay, then. Plan B. We'll go somewhere else."

Lexi was confused. "No. Jack. We can go. I'll be fine. I might need a stiff drink before I walk through the door though."

Jack reached down for her hand. "Lexi. I am working like crazy right now and the promise of tonight is the only thing that got me through this week. I'm not going to drag you to some event that might only upset you."

"But you're supposed to get an important award tonight."

Jack waved it off. "It's a plaque. I couldn't care less about that. I'd rather be with you."

Lexi's heart was being so fast that her brain couldn't keep up. She knew she was getting swept away by Jack, which she'd told herself dozens of times was a very bad idea. "I don't want you to have to rescue me again. You did that the day we met."

"Don't think of it that way. I did what anyone would have done. I know you would've done the same for me."

She wanted to think she had the nerve to save Jack, but she wasn't sure. She hadn't been tested like that before. "Where can we go if we don't go to Houston? We talked about getting out of Royal."

"I think we should go to Appaloosa Island."

"The construction site?"

Jack unleashed his hearty laugh. "No. I promise you that where we're going is a lot nicer than that."

Lexi looked down at her gown. "Whatever it is, I'm totally overdressed."

"No. You're perfect. I love seeing you in that. Not that I don't want you to be undressed later."

Heat rose in her cheeks. She swatted Jack on the arm. "You're bad."

"Or maybe very, very good." Jack's eyes glimmered. "Come on. We'll grab your bag and I'll speak to the pilot."

Lexi gathered her purse and phone charger from the front seat of her car as Jack brought her suitcase to the helicopter and briefly conferred with the pilot. Then he waved Lexi over and helped her on board. The cabin was even nicer than the one the bank owned, with white leather upholstery and enough room for six. Lexi took a center seat, with Jack next to her.

"Are we going to the hotel on Appaloosa?"

Jack shook his head as he buckled himself in. "I rented a house on the island a few weeks ago. It was too much to go back and forth all the time, and the owner is out of the country for at least six months. I figure that'll give me a prime spot for Soiree on the Bay." He swept her hair to one side and kissed her neck.

Lexi's eyes fluttered shut as she soaked up his warmth and the enticing brush of his skin against hers. It was the perfect reminder of why she was here—so she could finally have what she'd wanted since the moment she met this amazingly sexy man. "Jack, if you're going to kiss me like that, I don't care where we go. I only know that I'm ready to get there."

"I promise you it'll be spectacular." Jack reached for her hand as if it had become the most natural thing in the world. No, they weren't truly a couple, or boyfriend and girlfriend. She and Jack were just having fun. But as the helicopter took flight and Royal became a dot on the Texas landscape, it sure was starting to feel like something more than casual.

Six

Once again, Jack had proven himself to be full of surprises, pivoting from their Houston plan to one Lexi had never expected—an escape to Appaloosa Island. She had relished the thought of the five-star hotel, but there was something equally appealing about coming here. With little access from the mainland, they were essentially cut off from the world, if only for one night.

It was shortly after sunset when they arrived on the island, which Lexi realized left them the entire evening ahead. The mere thought sent goose bumps racing down her spine. She wanted Jack so bad, and there had been too much waiting. It felt as though she'd spent an eternity tasting his kisses on her lips, but never getting more. Perhaps that had been Jack's game all along, exercising his endless patience while she did nothing but squirm in her own skin. And right now, her desire for him was reaching a fever pitch, because all she could think about was getting him out of his suit, and him getting her out of this dress.

"Are we almost there?" she asked as they rode along in a small SUV that Jack had arranged for when the helicopter dropped them off. Although the island was far more developed on the western side, there was still very little in the way of streetlamps or normal city infrastructure. All around them was nothing but the slowly deepening blue of night, the softly moon-lit sway of tall palms in the wind and somewhere off in the distance, the Gulf. It was beautiful and serene. It reminded Lexi to take a breath and enjoy her time with Jack, even when she didn't want to wait anymore.

"Just a few more minutes." Jack slowed down and turned left on to a narrow gravel drive. The car pitched and rocked for several hundred feet, then they hit asphalt and the ride smoothed out.

Ahead, Lexi saw the outline of a massive white house. She knew that Rusty Edmond only let his closest friends, people of extreme means, build on the island. Still, Lexi hadn't expected such a grand structure. "Wow. This is it? What I can see is absolutely beautiful."

Jack pulled up and parked the car. "You will love this house. I have it rented for six months so I can be on the island for Soiree on the Bay, but honestly, I'm thinking about trying to buy it. The owner is an old friend of Rusty's, but he does so much business in Asia, that he's almost never here."

Lexi was interested in the backstory, but then again, she wasn't. She leaned over the center console and reached up, placing her finger against his warm lips. "Jack. If you don't take me inside and take off my clothes, I will never forgive you."

He smiled widely. Even in the dark, there was an unmistakable glimmer in his eyes. "I don't need to be asked twice. We'll leave the bags. I'll come out and get them later."

Or never, Lexi thought to herself. She did have some truly exquisite, very expensive lingerie in her bag, but she also felt like being naked would suffice, too. She didn't wait for Jack to open her door, hopping out of the car and hiking her dress up with one hand so she could hurry over to him. He took her hand and they ascended the full flight of stairs up to the house. After stealing a quick kiss, Jack entered a code on an electronic keypad.

When the lock clicked open, it was like a starting pistol. Lexi felt as though her heart was going to rocket out of her body. They stumbled through the front door, Jack closed it and her hands were all over him. Thank goodness she'd left her heels on or she'd be at a serious disadvantage here.

She kissed him without inhibition while she threaded her hands inside his jacket and pushed it from his shoulders to the floor. Her fingers scrambled to untuck his shirt, then went straight for the buttons. She flew through them like a woman on a mission. When she finally pulled the garment down his arms and was able to see his smooth bare chest and run her hands over it, it was like she'd unwrapped the best gift she could ever receive. As she'd hoped, he was pure muscled perfection, but feeling the warmth radiating from his skin and seeing the look on his face when he watched her touch him made it all the more real.

"You're amazing," she whispered, leaning in and kissing one of his defined pecs.

A deep groan escaped his throat. "You're the amazing one. And I want you closer to a bed." He swept her feet out from under her with what seemed like zero effort, carrying her up another flight of stairs. Then as he strode down a hall, she wrapped her arms around his neck, clinging to him and breathing in his smell, a heady mix of bourbon and cedar. He turned and angled her through a doorway and set her on the floor.

Lexi was in awe of the room, which had a generous king-size bed arranged with a perfect view of an entire wall of windows. Outside, the moon lit Trinity Bay, highlighting what was surely a beautiful vista by day. "It's so incredible, Jack," Lexi said, placing her hand on the wood molding between the windows. "This place is magical. I can't wait to see the view tomorrow."

Jack came up behind her and placed his hands on her shoulders. "I can't wait to see the view of you right now."

Lexi watched her reflection in the window as Jack slipped the straps of her dress from her shoulders and pulled them down her arms. Her nipples drew tight with the rush of cooler air against her skin. Watching him admire her body made the moment that much more intoxicating—she felt wanted. Desired. He kissed her shoulder one more time, then turned her around and dropped to his knees. Lexi kicked off her heels, leaving Jack's mouth at the perfect height to suck on one nipple and then the next. He looped his tongue around the hard bundle of nerves, sending zaps of electricity straight to her core. His generous hands cupped her breasts, lifting them higher and together in the center, while his eyes darkened as they raked over her.

Meanwhile, heat gathered between her legs and Lexi dug her fingernails into his shoulders, kissing the top of his head, holding his face to her bosom. Every kiss or lick he bestowed on her body felt like a message. *I want you.* If only he knew how badly she'd needed to feel like that.

She was intent on returning the sentiment, raising his face to hers and kissing him with as much raw passion as she'd ever shown. Even she marveled at her own boldness, the way she owned her movements and took what she wanted. Perhaps Jack had been right. Maybe she needed to get a few things out of her system. If so, being with him felt like it was opening the door on a whole new world, and Lexi was eager to explore it all.

Jack's hands were at her waist, but then he dropped them to her hips and pulled the dress down until it pooled around her feet. She was wearing only a pair of lacy red panties, a whisper of fabric between her and what she really wanted. Jack groaned when he sat back and looked at her, then stood and once again picked her up, taking only a few long strides before placing her on the bed.

Lexi stretched out on the cool linens, arching her back, and watching him study her body as he unzipped his pants. She raised one hand to her mouth, running a finger along her lower lip as he finished undressing and finally showed her everything she'd been waiting for. The moment was so worth marking—Jack was absolutely magnificent. Every inch of him was sculpted, and it was impossible to ignore the way he was so primed for her.

He stretched out next to her and Lexi rolled to

her side to kiss him. Her desire for him was too great—nothing seemed like it was happening fast enough, even when she wanted every moment to last. She hitched her leg up over his hip and got as close as she could to him, her apex hungry for his touch. He trailed his hand up and down the channel of her spine, then rolled to his back, pulling Lexi along with him until she was straddling his waist. She sat up and Jack molded his hands around her breasts, rubbing her nipples in tiny rotations with his thumbs. Lexi gasped at the pleasure and reminded herself to enjoy herself, to not be so impatient. Let Jack have control.

He gripped her rib cage and pulled her so close that her knees were nearly bracketing his chest. Then he bent down and drew one tight bud into his mouth, drawing circles with his tongue and sending Lexi into near oblivion as she felt bold enough to watch him. His lips against her skin, his dark eyes looking up at her—each inviting detail only stoked her desire for him. She wanted him with every molecule in her body.

Lexi rolled back onto the mattress and kneeled next to him, near his waist. She drew a line down the center of his chest, starting at the base of his throat, between his pecs, to his belly button and finally lower. Jack sucked in a sharp breath when she wrapped her fingers around his stiff erection. She was desperate to figure out what he liked, so at first, she took slow, gentle strokes. Jack mumbled his approval, something that sounded like *yes* over and over again. He seemed content, enjoying every instant of her touch, but when she tightened her grip, that made a very sexy rumble leave his throat. The satisfaction of having Jack at her command was far more than she'd bargained for. She felt strong. Powerful. And had never felt so alive.

"Do you have a condom?" Her voice was breathless and a little desperate. "I brought a box, but they're packed away with my toiletries. I guess that was stupid of me."

"Of course. I came prepared." He hopped up from the bed, giving Lexi the chance to watch his muscled frame in motion. Every inch of him was perfect, but his butt was particularly breathtaking.

Once again, she stretched out on the bed, swishing her hands against the silky linens as the seconds ticked by and anticipation boiled up inside her. Jack turned back to her, and his smile as he approached made her so dizzy that she nearly passed out. The only thing that kept her wits about her was the fight inside her—she would not be denied. She was finally going to have Jack.

That first glimpse of Lexi on the bed, wearing nothing more than sexy red panties and a knowing smile, ripped Jack's breath from his lungs. He'd imagined this a few times, but her beauty was so much more potent in person, far hotter than anything he ever could have dreamed up in his own head. Just kissing her in the foyer downstairs, with the knowledge that nothing was going to stop them, had been a lot to wrap his mind around. And now the moment was here.

He needed her with every inch of his body, but there was one part of him that was begging for her, so he tore open the foil packet and rolled on the condom. Jack was certain he'd never been so hard, was positive he'd never wanted a woman as much as he wanted Lexi right now, perhaps because he'd waited so long. But he also wanted to help her feel as good as she could possibly feel.

He stepped to the very end of the bed, nearest Lexi's feet. "I want you to do something for me."

"Anything."

How he loved the way she trusted him. "Clasp your hands and raise them up above your head."

Her sights narrowed on him, seeming skeptical, but she followed his directive, leaving her hands together up near the pillows. "I want to be able to touch you, Jack."

"Believe me, beautiful, I want that, too. But for now, I want you to think only about your own pleasure." He reached down and tugged her panties down her hips, past her knees and then her ankles, before dropping them to the floor.

Lexi wiggled in place, arching her back. "Jack. This doesn't seem fair."

He loved seeing her so impatient. "Oh, it will." With both hands, he urged her to spread her legs, then placed a knee on the bed. He drew his fingers along her inner thigh, then placed one of his knees on the bed so he had a better chance to slip his hand between her delicate folds and find her apex. She was so wet, so ready for him, it made yet another rush of blood race to his groin, amping up his need for her. He'd wait a little longer though.

Jack rubbed in gentle circles, studying her face as her eyes drifted shut then watched as she rolled her head to one side, her lips going slack. She was the most beautiful creature he'd ever seen, and that was not overstating the fact. He took immense pleasure in watching her reactions as she relaxed a little more and surrendered to his touch. With every circle he drew with his fingers, Lexi's breaths grew shorter. He knew she was close. That was all he wanted right now—just to push her to the edge, then tease her back from it. He knew from experience that it would make her climax that much more powerful.

Stretching out next to her, he pressed his lips to hers, his arms pulling her close. He listened for the changes in her breath as they were drawn back into another heavenly kiss, but she wasn't disappointed.

She wasn't even frustrated with him. In fact, she was on board with everything he did.

With a move Jack had not anticipated, Lexi pressed her hands against his chest, pushing him to his back. She climbed on top of him and Jack watched in utter fascination as she reached for his length and guided him between her legs. As she sank down onto him, a storm of heat threatened to swallow him whole. She fit perfectly around him, warm and soft. Being inside Lexi made his thoughts disjointed, so he focused on the physical sensations. The wait for this had been so worth it. They moved together, Lexi lowering her chest to his, not actually resting her body weight on him but instead rubbing her nipples lightly against his bare chest. No one had ever done that to him before. It nearly sent him over the edge.

Lexi's breaths were short once again. His own were rough and jagged. Pressure was building and he was in that intense place where you want to reach your destination, but you don't, because every second of the journey is so rife with pleasure. Lexi rolled her head to the side, eyes shut and pouty mouth slack, and he sensed she was close to surrendering to her peak.

Then she turned back to him and her eyes opened again, a wild and untamed green in the dark. She pressed her chest against his, and he was able to kiss her deeply and wrap his hands around her hips,

FREE BOOKS GIVEAWAY

2 FREE SIZZLING ROMANCE BOOKS!

2 FREE PASSIONATE ROMANCE BOOKS!

GET UP TO FOUR FREE BOOKS & TWO FREE GIFTS WORTH OVER $20!

We pay for everything!

dig his fingers into the lushness of her bottom. He thrust more forcefully, but it took very little to lift Lexi from the bed. The pent-up need coiled tight in his groin. It wouldn't be long before it would all break free. He pulled hard on her hips and rocked his pelvis so he could be even deeper inside her. That one change seemed to speed everything up as Lexi started to call out, then gasped for breaths, her mouth wide open as the orgasm hit her and she pulsed tight around him.

His own pleasure rocketed from the depths of his belly, a relentless cycle of tension winding up and letting go. Lexi gasped again and fell flat against his chest, kissing his neck over and over again. Jack rolled to his side and they were in each other's arms, breathless with contentment.

Lexi nuzzled his chest with her face, dotting his skin with delicate kisses. "That was amazing."

"It was." Jack's thoughts hadn't quite gathered yet, although he did know that he needed so much more of this incredible woman. "I want to remind you that we would be sitting in a stuffy hotel ballroom right now. And I'm positive this is so much better."

She kissed him softly. "I feel bad about that, Jack. You missed out on your award. Because of me and my pathetic history."

He shook his head. "Lexi. Stop saying things

like that. You've been through a hard time. It's not a reflection on you."

She blew out an exasperated sigh. "You're right. Bad habit."

"Are you doing okay, though? How long had you known that your ex got engaged?"

"About ten minutes before I saw you," she admitted. "Bianca called me while I was in the car."

"I'm glad she saw that and was able to warn you. Although, we would've just dealt with it if we'd had to run into him. I would've pulled you in my arms and laid a hot kiss on you to make him jealous."

Lexi laughed, but there was an edge of melancholy to it, too. "I don't think there's any making him feel like that. He's the one who wanted to split. He'd probably be relieved if I met a guy, got serious and got married so he didn't have to pay me alimony anymore. Well, that's not happening any time soon."

Jack's feelings could've been hurt by Lexi's words if he didn't understand why she felt that way. She'd been badly burned and would do anything to not experience that again. He still couldn't fathom how any man could walk away from Lexi, and he sensed that there was part of her that wondered the same thing. Jack wanted her to know that she wasn't alone in feeling rejected. She wasn't the only person who'd suffered such a heartache. "I have a confession."

"Then I want to hear it."

"Before I moved to Royal, I was engaged. My fiancée dumped me a few weeks before the ceremony. It's not quite the same as what you went through, and I have a feeling it must be far worse for the bride than the groom, but that was part of what made me jump in and say something to Ross the day we met. I know at least some of what it feels like, and I wanted to take that away."

Lexi looked deeply into his eyes. "Is that why you were okay with not going to Houston?"

"That was a bit more selfish, if I'm being honest. I have been looking forward to this all week, and I didn't want anything to get in the way of us being together, at least for a night."

Lexi smoothed her hand over Jack's chest, making desire bubble up inside him again. "What was your fiancée like? Had you been together a long time?"

Jack didn't think about Marcella very often now. It was a lifetime ago. He'd moved on. "She was nice enough to tell me that she wasn't really in love with me. At the time, it hurt like hell, but now I'm thankful. It never would've worked, and we both would've been miserable."

"I guess Brett was nice enough to call it off, too. I hadn't thought about it like that. I mostly thought about the mistakes I made."

"Like I said, Lexi, you need to stop focusing

on your missteps and focus on the good choices you've made."

"Like coming with you to Appaloosa Island for a night?"

Jack grinned wide. He hadn't been this relaxed or happy in a very long time. "You know, I've been thinking. There's no reason why you can't stay until Sunday night or even Monday morning. Even if they need me on the job site, I can pop over there easily, and being able to come back to you will be pretty amazing." He was struck by the thought of Lexi waiting for him, and of them spending more nights together. The idea suggested what might eventually be a serious relationship, and they weren't there yet, but he could imagine wanting to go there.

If only he could be sure that Lexi would want that, too.

Seven

Saturday morning, Jack tried to convince Lexi they should go swimming. In the bay.

"Jack. It's April. I don't care if we're in Texas. The water will *not* be warm." Lexi was wrapped up in nothing but a light blanket, comfortably perched in a white rocking chair as the sun warmed her face and ocean breezes blew back her hair. As far as she was concerned, she was going to finish her cup of coffee, then take Jack back upstairs and let him set her world on fire as many times as humanly possible. Last night had been epic, but that didn't mean they couldn't try for more.

He leaned against the railing, facing her and

wearing only a pair of board shorts and a smile. It wasn't fair. He was not only blocking out the sun, he was so spectacular, she could hardly think straight. "We'll run in for a few minutes. I promise it'll be exhilarating. Then we can get in the hot tub."

"There's a hot tub?"

Jack pushed off from the railing and pointed down to the floor below. "Right there."

Lexi got up from her seat to check it out for herself. Sure enough, down on the ground level was another deck, with an outdoor kitchen and spa. "How did I not see that?"

"I haven't given you the full tour." Jack placed his hand on her hip, tugging her closer. "We've been too busy."

Lexi rose up on to her tiptoes and kissed him. Even the most innocent of kisses felt hot right now. She knew what he was capable of now, and it made her hunger for him all the more. It was as if she'd been asleep her whole life, waiting for Jack's touch to awaken her. "I was hoping we could go back upstairs to the bedroom."

"A quick swim first? I promise I'll make it worth your time in the hot tub." He bounced his eyebrows up and down.

"Condoms and water don't mix."

"There are other things we can do."

That certainly sounded promising, and there was

no denying that every minute with Jack was an adventure. "You're lucky I brought a bathing suit."

"I would've been fine with you skinny-dipping."

"Hmm. I hadn't thought about that." It wasn't the worst idea in the world. A tiny number of people were on the island at any time, and there were no permanent residents. But Lexi could also imagine some massive yacht toddling by, possibly owned by someone her parents knew, and her flame red hair would stick out like a neon sign. Probably best not to take that chance. "I think I'll stick to my bikini, though. It's too cute to leave in the suitcase."

"Sounds like I win either way." Jack smiled, showing her those dimples she was somehow even more entranced by.

"Two minutes and I'll get changed."

"Sounds perfect. I'll grab some beach towels."

Lexi flitted upstairs and carefully sifted through the contents of her suitcase, pulling out her black bikini. She cast aside the blanket and put it on, stopping in the bathroom to brush her teeth. Glancing in the mirror, she couldn't help but notice the rosy glow in her cheeks and the way even her eyes looked brighter. Even better, she felt like she looked—like the day was full of possibilities, all because of Jack.

She met him down on the main floor, where the living room, kitchen and several other bedrooms were located. They walked out to the deck where she'd just been occupying the rocking chair and descended a staircase at the far end, taking them to the lower patio area, at the same level as the grass-topped dunes lining the beach. Hand in hand, they padded down the boardwalk and onto the pale gray sand. The wind whipped around them, and seagulls swooped out over the water while wisps of white clouds floated against a gauzy blue sky. Ahead, the deep azure of the Gulf was indeed inviting, but Lexi knew better than to jump right in. Her worries about it being cold were well-warranted. Depending on the currents, the water temperature could be in the sixties, a bit chillier than the air temp, which was in the low seventies at best.

They approached the waterline, where the sand was darker and the tide had revealed countless tiny shells. Looking down the beach in either direction, there wasn't another soul as far as the eye could see. The closest house, another stunning mansion, had to be at least a fifteen-minute walk away. Jack had been right. She could have skinny-dipped and no one would've known. They were all alone in what she saw as paradise.

Lexi squeezed his hand, feeling like she needed to mark the moment. She hadn't felt so free in a very long time. Possibly ever. Every worry she held so tightly in her head seemed insignificant right now. And it was all because of Jack. "Thank you for bringing me here. I'm sure our stay at the hotel in Houston would've been lovely, but this feels really special."

He turned to her and took her other hand, smiling and squinting at her as the sun hit his handsome face. "I'm so glad you said that. I was thinking the same thing."

"You're really serious about going in the water, aren't you?" Another gust of wind hit them, making goose bumps dot Lexi's arms and shoulders.

"I'm not going to force you."

However much she did not enjoy being cold, she wasn't about to be timid. There was this sense of adventure that followed Jack wherever he went, and she'd be stupid to pass up this chance to have an experience she might always remember. "I'm not a wimp."

"Of course not." He inched closer to the lapping waves, with Lexi in tow. "I usually run in up to my knees, dive under to get my head wet, swim out a few strokes and get out of the water."

Lexi could do that. No problem. And she wanted to show Jack that she could be bold, so she let go of his hand and did exactly what he suggested. The first few strides into the shallow water felt fine, so she went for it and dove in. She felt the cold first in her face, then her stomach, but it wasn't a shock—it was more of a pleasant jolt into the here and now. Her feet found the sandy bottom and she pushed off to surface, shaking her hair when she came up for air.

Jack was out of sight, and Lexi's heart was fiercely beating. "Jack?" She frantically looked all around her then screamed when she felt hands around her waist.

Jack rose out of the water like a god, pulling her into his arms and spinning her in the waves. "Well? What do you think?"

Honestly, the only thought that came to mind as he pressed his warm bare stomach against hers and water drops glistened on his face, was that he was perfect and she wasn't sure what she'd done to deserve this time with such a singular man. "It's amazing. *You're* amazing." She smashed her lips against his, her arms resting on his shoulders and her fingers digging into his hair. The kiss was just like the water in the bay—unpredictable and un-tamed, but nothing was forced. Everything felt right.

"Do you want to stay in?" Jack asked when he broke the kiss.

Lexi was out of breath. "Absolutely not. I'm freezing."

He laughed and scooped her up in his arms, showing off his strength by carrying her to shore. She could get so used to this. Then he gently set her feet on the sand and she grabbed the towels, tossing one to him and wrapping herself up in the other.

"Hot tub?" he asked.

"Yes."

They ran up the beach to the boardwalk, and after rinsing the sand from their feet, Jack opened up the hot tub cover and turned on the jets.

"Ooh. It feels a little hot after our swim," Lexi said, easing into the water.

Jack was less tentative, climbing right in and reclining in one of the seats. "You'll get used to it."

Lexi was already relaxed, but now that she was becoming accustomed to the warm water, she felt her muscles unwinding even more. "You're a smart man. You know that, right? I feel incredible right now."

Half a smile cracked at a corner of his mouth and she saw the familiar glimmer in his eyes. "I don't know about smart, but I'm sure I'm not dumb. All I want is whatever will make you happy."

Jack's words were everything she'd ever hoped to hear from a man. "That's so sweet of you. This whole trip has been wonderful. Thank you." The one thought persisting in her head was that the rules she'd given herself about not getting serious might not apply to Jack. He wasn't Brett. He wasn't Roger. He wasn't a man who'd broken her heart.

Jack held out his hand in invitation, his eyes heavy with desire. "Come here, beautiful."

She'd never taken a suggestion so readily. She slipped her hand into his and he tugged her closer through the water. His other hand cupped the side of her face, making her feel once again like she might melt. His touch was both firm and tender— how did he do that? How did he treat her with such regard while making it so clear that he wanted her?

Lexi leaned into him and shut her eyes, soaking up the instant when their mouths met and she could slip into the warmth of his kiss. Once again, that perfect mix of strong and soft. She tilted her head to the side and parted her lips, their tongues teasing and toying with each other. As each heavenly second ticked by, her body heat spiked hotter. She felt like she was on fire and not merely because she was up to her shoulders in hot water. Needing him, she placed a knee on the bench and straddled his lap.

He groaned into her mouth as her legs gripped his hips and she planted her elbows on his shoulders. Lexi dug her fingers into his hair, never allowing their kiss to break. She only wanted more. More heat. More intensity. She gently nipped his lower lip and she felt him get harder against her center. The faintest waves of his heady, masculine scent filled her nose, while his damp hair rubbed against the tender underside of her arms. He dragged his hands up and down her sides, squeezing and pressing into her skin like he couldn't get enough. It soon became evident that he wanted more, when he sneaked one hand to her back and tugged at the string across her back. As the garment came loose, Lexi pulled it over her head and tossed it on to the deck.

"That's so much better," she muttered, pressing her breasts against his bare chest. Her nipples tightened at that small bit of friction. The need inside her rolled to the boil and she rocked her hips, grinding against him, needing the gratification of his touch. "I need you, Jack."

He moved his mouth to her ear. "I need to hear you say that." It sounded like he was on board, but he still held on to her so tight that it seemed like he didn't share her immense sense of urgency.

"Then let's get out."

"In a minute." Jack flattened his hand against Lexi's belly and slid it down into the front of her bikini bottoms.

She gasped when his talented fingers found her apex. Her eyes slammed shut, and she pitched forward, nestling her face in Jack's neck. He continued in determined circles, not stopping, only changing the pressure. The tension in her body doubled, then doubled again.

"Kiss me, Lexi."

The deep tenor of his voice was only more of a turn-on. She dragged her cheek across his stubble and kissed him with as much unbridled enthusiasm as she could muster. He met her effort, and it was like they were trying to outdo each other. The only difference was that Lexi was right at the brink, her attention spiraling between the sensations—the kiss and the spellbinding action of his hand.

The peak rolled right over her, causing her to cry out and knock back her head as she dug her fingers into his shoulders. He stilled his hand, then dragged it along the center of her torso, between her breasts, then back down, as her body shuddered with the exquisite pleasure. As those final waves receded, she sought the comfort of his arms. Lexi could be as vulnerable as she wanted with Jack, no strength to speak or stand, and it didn't matter. She'd never felt safer.

There was something about watching Lexi unravel, with the beauty of Appaloosa Island all around them, that made Jack impossibly happy. Yes, he was overwhelmed by her beauty, but he was equally blown away by the difference in her since they'd arrived. Lexi was unwinding here, not worried about what anyone thought about her. She wasn't fixated on the forces in their world that thought the two of them as a couple was a bad idea. And the joy that brought him scared him a bit— he hadn't realized that he'd been waiting for her to show him a sign that there was a chance for them to have more.

Of course, Jack wasn't thinking about those things either when he had Lexi at his mercy. He was only relishing what she was at her core—a sensitive, sexy and smart woman. A person who had been read wrong by a lot of people. Jack had been underestimated many times in his, life and he knew exactly how much it hurt. Lexi wasn't the poor little rich girl people gossiped about, and if she *was* that, he sure didn't see her that way. Part of him wanted to rage against everyone who had ever whispered about her behind her back. Another part of him thought those people weren't worth the trouble.

Lexi spread her hand across Jack's chest and kissed his wet skin. "I need to take care of you now."

As appealing as that was, he needed to clear his head. He'd told himself that he had zero problem with things staying casual, just as Lexi wanted. Now he wasn't so sure, not when his only thought was to keep her on Appaloosa forever. That didn't sound like a noncommittal frame of mind. "You know, I'm starving. Maybe we can grab some lunch first. Then I'll have my strength back."

Lexi narrowed her eyes, seeming suspicious, but ultimately nodded in agreement. "I guess I'm pretty hungry, too." She climbed out of the hot tub, wrapped herself up in a towel and grabbed her bikini top from the deck.

Jack closed up the hot tub and they headed upstairs to the kitchen. He didn't bother getting dressed, content to walk around in his swim trunks, but Lexi ran up to the bedroom, quickly returning barefoot and wearing a black-and-white-checkered sundress with skinny straps. She had no makeup on, and her hair was pulled back in a high ponytail that really showed off the natural color in her cheeks. This was not the everyday Lexi, with her flawless appearance and designer wardrobe, and Jack knew for a fact that most people never saw her this way. He felt damn lucky to be with both versions of her.

It was really nice to make lunch together, just some sandwiches with fixings he had stocked the fridge with a few days ago. Lexi made an amazing side salad with a vinaigrette she whipped up on the fly, and they sat out on the deck while they ate, just watching the waves, breathing in the salt air, laughing and talking. Jack couldn't think of a time when he'd been this at ease with a woman, and so soon. He had to remind himself that he and Lexi had hardly known each other for two weeks. But that didn't even seem possible. Because he felt like he'd known her forever.

"How's the search for a place to live going?" Jack asked.

"It isn't. I've been so crazy busy at work I haven't had a chance to call the real estate agent. I guess I'd better get on that."

He was surprised she hadn't even started the process. For someone so eager to get out from under her parents' control, he thought she would've set the wheels in motion by now. "Well, whenever you're able to go look at some places, I'll be happy to go with you if you want. I can spot poor construction from a mile away."

"That would be great! Bianca has offered to go with me, too, but she's more worried about how far away I'll be living from her. She'd like me to be close."

Although that hinted at more familial interference, he appreciated her bond with Bianca. He had a similar relationship with his sister Angie. "What do your parents think about all of that?"

"They're happy with me being in the guesthouse, to be honest. But I think they're just being protective. They're convinced I'm going to fall apart at some point, and I think my dad in particular likes the idea of being the one to pick up the pieces."

It wasn't hard to imagine Winston wanting to fill that role. "How are things with your dad? I still feel bad about that night at the TCC. I'm really sorry I reacted that way." Now that Jack had long since cooled off, he knew that he'd been stewing over the way Winston had treated him for years. He'd let that boil over that night, and it wasn't fair to Lexi.

"To be honest, they're strained. I'm mad at him for the way he treated you, Jack, and he knows that. But he's so stubborn that he won't admit that he was wrong. He might never admit it."

"I bear at least some of the responsibility for what happened that night. I could've kept my cool."

Lexi shook her head and looked at him with determination blazing in her eyes. "No. He started it. As far as I'm concerned, the blame all lies with him."

That didn't sit well with Jack—if he could take some of the heat for the situation, it would lessen the tension. Hopefully he could find a way to have a chat with Winston and smooth things out. "All I'm saying is that there are two sides to every story, and I'm not afraid to own up to my part in this one."

"I appreciate that. Seriously." Lexi reached over and traced her finger up and down his forearm. "You know, Jack, I have to say thank you for bringing me here. I think this was exactly what I needed. It's been fun and relaxing, and we get along so well."

"You're most welcome. I couldn't agree more about all of that. Especially the last part."

Her face lit up with a smile. "It's funny, isn't it?"

"How so?"

She shrugged and looked out over the water. "We're very different people. We come from such different backgrounds. And yet we naturally get along."

"People don't have to be the same to be compatible."

"I know. I'm just glad that something for once is easy. That I don't have to try to be something I'm not around you."

Jack was doing his best to take her words in the spirit in which he believed they were intended. "You never have to pretend around me, Lexi. In fact, I'd rather see the unvarnished version of you."

She turned back to him and smiled sweetly. "And that's what's so awesome about you, Jack. As a woman who just spent fifteen years with a man who expected perfection, it's a refreshing change of pace."

Jack decided he would leave it at that. He wasn't going to get caught up in semantics or dig for more. Lexi was happy right now. She liked that the two of them together, at least on Appaloosa Island, was a simple proposition. He could be content with that. For the time being.

Lexi got up out of her chair and reached for his empty plate. "I'll clean up the kitchen and then we can go upstairs?"

"Sounds perfect."

Once the dishes were loaded into the dishwasher, they headed upstairs. Jack decided to hop in the shower to wash off any residual saltwater from their swim. When he was done, he dried himself off and walked into the bedroom with the towel wrapped around his waist, but he didn't get far. There on the bed was Lexi, leaning against the headboard, wearing a sexy black lace negligee that accentuated every enticing part of her. It was cut low in the front, drawing attention to her luscious breasts,

BLUE COLLAR BILLIONAIRE

and impossibly short, showing off her beautiful legs. Her hair tumbled across her shoulders, and the clever grin on her face told Jack everything he needed to know.

His body responded immediately, every muscle drawing tight with the need for her. But as he cast aside the towel and set a knee on the bed to get closer to her, he knew this was about to be way more than sex. He was falling for Lexi. And there wasn't a damn thing he could do about it.

Eight

Jack and Lexi couldn't bear to leave Appaloosa on Sunday, so they said their goodbyes before dawn on Monday morning, in the parking lot of the airstrip. "This weekend was amazing." Lexi wanted to say more, to let him know exactly how much it had meant to her, but she also didn't want to lay it on too thick. She knew her own tendencies too well...that she was apt to go overboard. *Slow and steady*, she reminded herself. *You and Jack have plenty of time.*

"It was the most fun I've had in a really long time," Jack said. "I feel bad dropping you off so early. The sun just came up. That doesn't seem quite right."

"I don't mind at all. You know, it'll probably be

good for me to get into the office early this morning. Before my dad arrives."

Jack nodded. "Speaking of work, I need to get home, change, pack and then head back to the island. We have a big week ahead of us."

Lexi was going to be so glad when the festival construction was over and she and Jack would have fewer obstacles to spending time together. "I'll let you go." The bittersweet tone of her voice said it all—she didn't want to do that. Despite her trepidation about getting involved with a man, there was one fact she couldn't deny. This weekend had not been enough.

Jack leaned down and pressed his forehead against hers. "I don't want to go, if that makes you feel any better."

Lexi couldn't help but smile. "It does make me feel better. A lot better." She raised her lips to his. Even now, when they'd kissed millions of times, he still managed to make it incredibly exciting. "I'll see you on Saturday, right? Angie's birthday at your house?"

"Yes. Absolutely. Remember your bathing suit. We'll be in the pool. I like the one you wore on the island."

"At your sister's birthday party? I'm thinking I'll go with something a little more conservative." She kissed him again.

"Party pooper."

"You'll get to see the black bikini again. But it'll be a time when it's only the two of us." Lexi realized that she and Jack were officially making plans—lots of them. Part of that thrilled her, but it also made fertile ground for the seed of doubt in her head, the one that worried things were going too fast.

"That sounds wonderful."

Jack kissed her one last time and then Lexi climbed into her car, stopping to wave goodbye to him when she pulled out of her parking space. As she drove off, she realized that she felt like she was walking on air. She knew this feeling…she'd felt it with Roger once and with Brett twice. Infatuation. Preoccupation. The start of the feelings that sometimes led to love. But she couldn't afford to be starry-eyed about it this time around.

Lexi strolled into the Alderidge Bank office by eight o'clock, arriving before most of the executive staff, including her dad. She loved being at work before everyone else. It gave her a sense of autonomy she rarely enjoyed when her father's presence was impossible to ignore.

It was too early to call most people, but she fired off several emails—one to Lila with the Chamber of Commerce to see if Lexi could get the first jump on any upcoming events the town might be holding. Another message went to the real estate agent Bianca suggested. She even sent along some links to a few houses she was interested in—homes that were closer to her sister, but on the opposite end of town from Pine Valley. Her last message went to Mandee Meriweather from the local gossip TV show *Royal Tonight!* It wasn't like Lexi to encourage tabloid journalism, but she did want to talk about the bank's involvement in Soiree on the Bay. She was serious about positioning the bank as hip and accessible, rather than the ultraexclusive image her father had cultivated.

What Lexi hadn't counted on was getting a phone call from Mandee less than five minutes after she sent the email.

"Lexi Alderidge. I am so excited you contacted me. I'd love to do an interview with you." There was something about Mandee's tone that sent a shiver up Lexi's spine. The reporter was known to be a bit of a shark, and from her tone she smelled blood in the water.

Still, Lexi felt as though she had to play along. "Oh, great. We can talk about the bank's involvement in Soiree on the Bay. Maybe get one of the people from the festival advisory board to join me."

"We can talk about that, but what I *really* want to hear about is your relationship with Jack Bowden. There's quite a buzz around town."

"There is?" If that was the case, Lexi was oblivious to it, but she'd spent very little time running around town, and of course, she and Jack had just disappeared for nearly three whole days.

"Lexi, can I record this? Then I can add our conversation to tonight's show."

"I'd really prefer it if you didn't. I'd rather talk about the festival."

"Soiree on the Bay will be a hot topic of conversation when it happens, but until then, I think people want to hear your story, Lexi. It doesn't have to be a negative thing. People want to hear about you moving on after your divorce, and that whole messy situation with Brett Harston leaving you at the altar." Mandee cleared her throat. "And then there's the latest story about your ex-husband getting engaged."

Lexi's stomach lurched. Had she opened Pandora's box by contacting Mandee? It sure felt like it. She had to protect herself, but more than anything, she felt she needed to shield Jack from this, as well. "Jack and I are friends. That's all I'm going to say about that. Thank you for the offer of an interview, but I'll have to pass for now. Let me know when you want to talk about Soiree on the Bay."

"That's disappointing, Lexi."

"Sorry. I don't want to talk about my personal life right now."

"Call me if you change your mind. And in the meantime, have fun with Jack. He's a hottie. I know fifty women who would *love* to be with him."

Lexi knew she was lucky to have caught Jack's eye. However, she didn't enjoy the reminder. "Bye, Mandee."

"See you around, Lexi."

"I hope not," Lexi muttered to herself after she'd ended the call. She looked out the window of her office, wondering what Jack was doing, if he was out on Appaloosa Island by now. Their weekend together still fresh in her mind, she couldn't help but wish she was back there with him. Having that respite from everyday life had been amazing. And the call with Mandee was a reminder of how nice it was to get away.

A knock came at her office door, followed quickly by her father opening it and strolling inside. "Good morning, Alexis."

Lexi got up from her desk to greet her father. "Good morning. Also, you should wait until someone says, 'come in' before you walk into their office."

"I own the bank, Lexi. I own that door. And that desk. In fact, I own everything you see."

Lexi fought her inclination to roll her eyes. "I realize that, Dad. But it's still the polite thing to do." She returned to her chair and took a seat. "Do you need something from me?"

"I was disappointed to see you were gone all weekend and didn't think to tell us that you wouldn't be home. Your mother and I were worried sick. We called Bianca. She told us where you went."

Lexi wished her sister was a little less open with their parents. She could've covered for Lexi and said that she'd gone to a spa for the weekend or something less controversial than spending several days with a man her father didn't seem to like. "I'm sorry, but I'm thirty-eight years old. I didn't think I needed to report to you."

"While you're staying on the family compound, I'd appreciate the courtesy of an update. It's only natural that we would want to know where you are and that you're safe."

He wasn't wrong, but this was certainly cause for ramping up the timeline on moving out. "I'm sorry, Dad. It won't happen again. Plus, you won't have to deal with it for too much longer. I've reached out to a real estate agent. I'm hoping she can show me a few houses this week."

"There's no reason to rush. You're welcome to stay in the guesthouse as long as you want."

"I appreciate that. I do. But I need my independence. Do you realize I've never lived in my own place? I went from living at home, to a dormitory, to Roger, and then back home. I need a house of my own."

Her father nodded and stuffed his hands into his pants pockets. Lexi always worried when her dad got quiet. It usually meant he was mad, or at the very least unhappy. "Are you going to admit to me that you spent the weekend with Jack Bowden?"

Here we go. Apparently, they were about to have this discussion. "I don't have to admit anything. I'm not embarrassed. Yes, Jack and I went away. He's working incredibly hard on the Soiree on the Bay project and only has time on the weekends."

"Is it serious?"

Lexi shook her head adamantly, even when she wasn't certain her response warranted that much of a definitive slant. "It's not."

"Why do I feel like you're just telling me what I want to hear?"

Because I am? Because I don't know what else to say. Even I don't know what's going on between me and Jack. "It's the truth. I thought you'd be happy to hear those two things match up."

"I don't want you getting in too deep, Lexi. A guy like Jack is okay for dating. But you know, when the time comes, you'll want to set your sights a little higher."

Lexi knew very well that her father had some pigheaded ideas lodged deep inside him. But she was still surprised when she heard those things come out. She'd listened to this speech as it pertained to Brett many times. And she wasn't going to make the mistake of nodding her head like a good daughter and letting him get away with this close-mindedness again. "Dad. You don't know Jack. I can assure you that he's of the highest character. He treats me better than any man has ever treated me, and that includes my husband." It was the truth. Jack regarded her like she was a queen. And when they were together, she never doubted that she was his sole focus. "And honestly, you should be thanking Jack because he saved me from some epic embarrassment on Friday night. We were going to a charity event in Houston and Roger was going to be there. With his new fiancée. Jack changed our plans, even though he was supposed to get an award."

Her dad cast a dubious look her way. "My guess is that he had other objectives."

"Dad. Listen to yourself. Jack's instinct was to protect me. If anyone should appreciate that, it's you."

"I'll decide what's worth appreciating."

Lexi decided this was going nowhere. She got up from her desk, walked past her dad and waited at the door, hoping he'd take the hint that he was cordially invited to leave. "If you don't mind, I should get to work. I'm expecting a call from Lila with the Chamber of Commerce. There's an arts fair this fall I think we should sponsor."

"Arts fair? I'm not sure that attracts the sort of people who might want to bank with us."

As much as Lexi was tired of this conversation, this was the perfect illustration of his troublesome attitudes. "And that's the problem. When a man like

Jack Bowden, who is hardworking, honest and owns a solid business, walks away from our bank feeling as though he isn't welcome, that spells trouble for our business. We need to be welcoming, not sitting in an ivory tower."

Her dad opened his mouth to respond, but just as fast, he closed it.

"Dad. Whatever it is you have to say to me, come out with it. I'm tired of tiptoeing around these things. I know you feel like I'm trying to change everything, but I only want you to open your eyes. I love you, and I don't want to see your life's work go down the drain. But I think it will if you don't take the time to consider that the old way of working was never a very good way."

He sighed and wandered over to the window. "Do you ever feel old, Lexi?" He turned back to her. "Because I do. And every time we have this conversation, I feel a little bit more so. I've been in charge of things for so long that it's hard to let go. And I can't help it. I feel better when I'm in charge of things."

"You're still in charge, Dad. I'm just steering you in a slightly different direction. One that I think will seal your legacy and the future of the bank. That's all I want."

He smiled thinly. "Do you know what I want?"

"I don't."

"For you and me to be able to work together, happily."

"Okay. That's going to require some flexibility on your part."

"I'm beginning to see that." He strolled back to the door. "And I will try. I will."

Lexi wasn't sure she should broach the other subject looming overhead, but now seemed as good a time as any. "I would feel better if you and Jack could make another run at getting to know each other."

"I thought you said it wasn't serious."

"It isn't," she admitted. "But I like him a lot, and I'd like to date him. I'd like my dad to know and appreciate a man I'm involved with."

"Since when does my opinion matter on the subject of your love life?"

Lexi laughed. She couldn't help it. That was the only obvious reaction to his absurd question. "Since forever. I don't feel like you ever approve of my choices. And I'm tired of feeling like that."

"The divorce wasn't your choice."

"But you blame me for it, don't you?"

He frowned and marched right up to her, gently caressing her shoulder. "Never, Lexi. Roger hurt you. I would never blame you for that."

"Seriously?"

"Seriously. I only want you to be happy. Roger made you unhappy, and that makes him the wrong person for you. That is the extent of my opinion on the matter." He let go of his grip on her and strode back to the door. "As for Jack, let's play it by ear."

It was late on Monday night when Jack arrived back at the Appaloosa house to grab a few hours of sleep. Just like when he and Lexi had done when they'd first arrived Friday, Jack practically stumbled inside. He sat on the stairs in the foyer and untied his work boots, casting them aside. He was exhausted. Dead on his feet. It was past ten o'clock, and if he didn't get to bed soon, that exhaustion was only going to get worse tomorrow.

He trudged up the stairs and down the hall to his bedroom, immediately confronted by the memory of his weekend with Lexi. They'd made love in nearly every corner of this room. It used to be that he would go to the window and look out at the water, but now he was struck by the mental image of the first time he saw Lexi naked, her luscious body reflected in the glass and lit by the soft glow of the moon. And then there was the bed, where time and place had meant virtually nothing because they were so wrapped up in each other. Even this room smelled like her, and that made the rest of the workweek staring him down that much more depressing. He wasn't sure he could make it without seeing her. And that was a worry in its own right. He wasn't supposed to get in so deep with Lexi.

Damn. What kind of spell was this woman casting over him?

To wash away his day, he walked into the bath and turned on the shower, then shucked his dirty work clothes and stepped inside. As the warm spray hit his back and shoulders, the temperature in the room began to rise. Jack closed his eyes and made a conscious decision to relax, but that made the visions of Lexi that much more real, especially in the shower, where everything was hot. And wet. As he lathered himself up, he couldn't stop thinking about her, about kissing her, touching her and being inside her. His entire body went tight at the thought, then with a rush, the blood in his body seemed to head straight for his groin.

He opened his eyes and looked down, confronted with his own arousal. Logic said he could easily satisfy this urge on his own, but the truth was that the mere thought of Lexi made his chest ache. Rinsing, he wondered if she would be up for a late-night phone call. *All I can do is try*, he thought as he turned off the shower.

He grabbed a towel and dried off his chest and shoulders, then stretched out on the bed and called Lexi.

"Hello?" she answered, her voice light and bubbly.

"Hello, beautiful." He nearly growled out his response. One word from her and his whole body felt like it was going to explode.

"I'm surprised you called. I figured you would be too busy. Or sleeping. I didn't want to bother you."

Jack stared up at the ceiling, but in his mind, all he saw was Lexi—her gorgeous red hair and bright green eyes. "You couldn't bother me if you tried. What are you doing?"

"Just getting ready for bed. I was going to read for a bit then catch up on sleep. Somebody kept me up all weekend."

Jack laughed and closed his eyes, luxuriating in Lexi's sweet, sultry voice. Indeed, they hadn't slept much over the course of the weekend, but rest was the last thing he cared about right now. "Have you already dressed for bed?"

"That's sort of a weird question."

"You wouldn't say that if you knew what state I'm in right now."

"And what would that be?"

Jack was having a hard time putting this into words. How he wished she was here, in some mind-blowing lingerie, and he could take off every enticing stitch of it and make love to her. "On the bed. No clothes. And hard."

"Oh. I see…"

Lexi wasn't giving him much to work with here, and he couldn't help but feel like he was standing on a precipice, staring down his own future. If he leaped, would she follow? Or would she say it was too much? *Life is too short to second-guess yourself, Jack.* "I swear, Lexi. One step into this bedroom and all I could do was think about you and how badly I want you. How amazing our weekend was. And how much I can't wait to do it again."

"That's so sweet, Jack. Truly."

It still felt like she was missing the point. He wanted to be talking to the Lexi who was bold and not shy. He wanted her to show him just how uninhibited he knew she could be. "I'm not trying to be sweet, Lexi. I'm trying to seduce you. I want you to undress and tell me what you're doing. Tell me what you're feeling."

Several moments of quiet played out on the other end of the line. The wait was excruciating. "Of course I will. Anything you want."

"Just tell me everything, okay?" Jack put his phone on speaker and laid it next to him on the bed.

"Got it. Yes. Hold on." In the background, there was the sound of drawers or doors opening and closing. "Okay. I took off my dress. I'm going to climb up on my bed now."

"Does that mean you're naked?"

"No. Of course not. I still have my bra and panties on. I know you like lingerie."

Jack swallowed back a groan, and slid his hand down his stomach, but he didn't touch himself yet.

He wanted to savor this. "Tell me more. The color. What they feel like."

"They're dark purple. Like a plum in the middle of summer. They're silky soft, but they have lace, too. At the edges."

Jack saw the whole scene in his mind's eye. "I can imagine," he said gruffly. "I'm sure you look absolutely ravishing. I can't wait until I can touch you again. Until I can taste your skin again."

Lexi hummed her approval over the phone. "I can't wait either, Jack. You're making me want you so bad right now."

"How bad?"

She nearly made him rocket into space when she told him how just hearing his voice made her nipples hard. How she wished he could touch every inch of her. He wrapped his hand around himself, but it was Lexi's velvety fingers he felt against his skin. So warm. So perfect. Exactly what he wanted.

The pressure built as she narrated taking off her panties, when she told him that she was touching herself but imagining it was him. Even with her heavenly scent all over the pillows, the experience wasn't the real thing, but for right now, it was as close as he was going to get. The tension in his hips was so tight he felt like he might snap in half. He told her how he imagined her kisses, and she moaned into the phone, making it clear that she was near her own climax. Jack silently begged for release and his body answered, the pleasure roaring through his body like a rockslide down a mountain face. Thankfully, Lexi followed almost right after him. He sank into the mattress, breathless.

"Lexi? Are you there?"

She giggled. "I am. I'm sure you're sick of me saying this, but you are full of surprises, Jack. When you called tonight, I was not expecting *that*."

Jack's chest, neck and face flushed with heat. Even after their wickedly hot phone call, he wanted more. "It's all you, Lexi. Just thinking about you and hearing your voice gets me all worked up."

Nine

Saturday afternoon, on her way to Jack's house for his sister's birthday party, Lexi was unbelievably nervous. Her outfit wasn't making things any better. She shifted in the driver's seat, tugging at the dress that she'd agonized over. Was it too dressy? Too casual? Would his sister hate her? She wasn't sure how her brain made that particular leap, but it kept doing it.

With only ten minutes until she'd arrive at Jack's house, Lexi decided to make a desperate call to Bianca. She needed a cheerleader right now.

"Hey, you," her sister answered.

"Help me calm down."

"I'm currently quizzing Maisie for her history test, so it'll have to be fast."

As if Lexi needed more pressure. "I'm on my way to Jack's. He's hosting a birthday party for his younger sister. His best friend Rich will be there, too."

"And you're worried they aren't going to like you?"

Thank goodness Bianca understood her so well. "Oh, my God, yes."

"This is not good."

"What? You're supposed to be reassuring me right now that everything is going to be okay. And hurry up. According to the GPS, I'm going to be there in five minutes."

"I meant it's not good that you're worried. If this wasn't serious, we wouldn't be having this conversation. And since you decided to call me, I have no other choice than to assume that you're getting in deep with Jack."

Lexi's navigation system chimed in. *In five hundred feet, turn left. Destination will be on your right.*

"I don't know how many times I have to tell you this. It's not serious. We're having fun."

"Does the way you feel right now seem like fun? Because it sure doesn't sound like it."

Lexi made the turn onto the private drive leading up to Jack's house. Up ahead, at the top of the hill, sat a beautiful sprawling home, charcoal gray with exposed dark wood beams and creamy white trim, surrounded by green rolling vistas as far as the eye could see. Of course, Jack would have a show-stopper of a home—she wasn't sure why she'd expected anything less. "I don't know what I'm doing, to be honest. And I have zero time to figure it out because I'm basically here."

"Fine. Then let me give you some quick advice. Have a glass of wine. Don't bring up anything too serious. And more than anything, be yourself. Either they'll like you or they won't. That's not up to you to decide."

If only it was so simple. Lexi pulled up and parked in an open space off to the side of the garage. There were two other cars parked outside—a big black pickup truck and a silver mini SUV. Luckily, she was apparently one of the first to arrive. It would be easier if she could ease into this rather than walk into a house full of strangers. "Okay."

"You don't sound convinced."

"I'm not. But I'll do my best."

"If this isn't serious, don't take it seriously," Bianca said. "I think that's the best way to go."

Lexi thanked her then hung up, her stomach wobbling with unease. She grabbed her bag and the gift she'd bought for Angie and climbed out of the car just as Jack stepped out the front door onto his wraparound front porch. That one glimpse of him and his broad smile made all the worry evaporate. She hadn't seen him since early Monday morning at the airstrip, and although they'd talked on the phone every night all week, it didn't come close to matching the sight of him in person. She nearly ran to him, even in heels, flinging her arms around him, or as close as she could get considering their size difference. For Jack's part, he threaded his arms under Lexi's and her feet left the ground when he lifted her for a kiss.

"It's so good to see you," he said.

"Nice to see you, too," Lexi murmured.

From somewhere behind him, someone cleared their throat.

Jack whipped around. "Oh, Angie. I'd like you to meet Lexi. Lexi, this is Angie."

Jack's sister stepped forward, tall like he was, but willowy. Her hair was a shade darker brown than Jack's, and she had a natural beauty accentuated by her strong features, wide sable eyes and full lips. She was dressed in a flowing red sundress and flat sandals. "Finally, I meet the famous Lexi. Thank you for coming." She sized her up, then offered a hug.

Lexi was relieved, figuring no one hugs a person they think they might ultimately hate, and she eagerly accepted the embrace. "I'm glad we finally get to meet. Happy birthday." She handed over the gift, again feeling uncertain.

"Thank you. I'll open this later. With the rest of the presents."

A very tall man Lexi didn't know emerged through the front door. "I've been looking for you guys."

"Rich, come meet Lexi," Jack said, waving him over.

So, this was Rich, Jack's best friend. He towered over Lexi, just like Jack, nearly as muscle-bound and broad-shouldered. He offered his hand. "I've heard a lot about you."

She hoped that was a good thing. "It's great to finally put a face with the name."

Several more cars pulled up into the driveway. "I should go greet my guests."

Angie grabbed Lexi's hand. "Go. Lexi and I will get to know each other."

"It's your birthday," Jack said. "Don't you think you should come with me?"

"They're your friends, Jack. Remember, I'm the new girl in town. I can meet them later. This might be the only chance Lexi and I get to talk about you."

Jack slid his sister a skeptical look and put on his sunglasses. "Be nice."

"I always am."

Lexi followed Angie inside, into a soaring open foyer. Off to one side was a formal dining room, and on the other side there seemed to be a study. Straight ahead was a wide corridor, leading them to the back of the house. At the end of the hall, the space opened up into a great room with a gourmet kitchen to the right, with pale gray cabinetry, white marble countertops and a beautiful glass mosaic backsplash in a muted color scheme. On the left was a living room with the largest sectional sofa and entertainment center Lexi had ever seen. Everything about this house was like Jack—the furniture was big, the ceilings were tall, but the casual elegance of the decor put a person at ease right away.

"Come on and get a load of the pool." Angie led the way to the windows, which overlooked an expansive patio area and large pool with waterfalls, natural clusters of stone, and even a waterslide. It was a true oasis, but it was also a place to play and have fun.

Lexi didn't pin any of Jack's worth on his financial status, but there was still a part of her that wanted her dad to see all of this. It might change his mind. "It's beautiful," she said to Angie.

The other woman nodded. "My brother put his heart and soul into this house. But he does that with everything."

"You two are close, aren't you? You'd have to be to move to a new town and start over, just so you could be in the same place."

Angie leaned against the wood frame between windows. "It was a little more than that. Not sure if Jack told you, but I just went through a divorce.

I feel a little pathetic since I'm only twenty-nine. I figured I'd at least get to thirty before my life started falling apart."

Lexi's heart went out to Jack's sister. She understood everything Angie was saying. "I was married for fifteen years before my husband dumped me. That's a lot of time, and it's hard not to feel like I wasted it by being with the wrong person."

"Did you have kids?" Angie asked.

Lexi shook her head. "No."

"Me neither."

"I wanted them, but my husband didn't, and I never forced the issue. I know people say that it's better to have not had children when you go through a divorce, but it's still a big regret of mine. I wish I had spoken up for what I wanted."

Angie looked back in the direction of the front door. Jack was walking in with a group of five or six people. She returned her attention to Lexi. "The flip side of that is you tell him exactly what you want and it turns into a big fight. That was the case for me."

Lexi hadn't considered that possibility. She'd had several months to reflect back on her marriage to Roger, and she'd worried many times that she'd allowed herself to be a doormat. "I guess we've both been through the wringer."

Angie drew a deep breath through her nose. "Definitely. The question is where do we go from here? I don't know about you, but I'm not ready to tie myself to another guy."

Lexi truly felt put on the spot, but she had to be honest. "I'm not ready either, but I do like your brother a lot. We have so much fun together."

"I don't know that it's possible to not have fun with my brother."

From across the room, a woman Lexi didn't know was laughing and grabbing Jack's biceps. She did her best to tamp down her jealousy, but it was next to impossible.

"Case in point," Angie said, with a nod toward the woman. "The ladies find him endlessly entertaining."

Lexi couldn't help but think about the comment Mandee Meriweather had made about how she knew fifty women who would love to date him. Jack hadn't talked at all about his romantic past, other than to share the story of his own failed engagement. "You've probably seen him with lots of different women."

Angie twisted her lips into a bundle, as if she was considering how much to say. "I don't want to lie to you."

"It's okay. I suspected as much."

"Let's just say he hasn't taken anyone seriously since his fiancée dumped him," Angie confided.

"He told me about that. One of those odd things we have in common."

"If it makes you feel any better at all, I haven't seen him be so over the moon with a girlfriend in a long time."

"I don't know that I've earned the girlfriend designation," Lexi said. "Jack definitely left that out when he introduced me to you and Rich."

Angie frowned. "Really? I hadn't noticed."

Lexi had, right away. But she didn't want to make a big deal about it, especially since the other woman would likely bring it up with Jack. "It's nothing. And believe me, I'm not pushing for the label. I'd rather just be Lexi, and he can be Jack. That's enough."

But was that true? *Was* it enough? Lexi glanced over at Jack and caught his eye, his lips turning up in a smile before he returned his attention to the conversation he was having. She couldn't ignore the way she was happier when she was around him, the way he made everything better and brighter. It was like there was a big flashing sign in her face, telling her to not mess this up. She only wished the timing was different, that she'd made more headway with being her own person and standing on her own two feet before Jack came along.

"Come on," Angie said. "We should probably go join the rest of the party."

"Lead the way."

Although playing the role of host had been a big job, tackling everything from ordering Angie a cake to organizing the guest list, Jack still found it a welcome respite to have a weekend away from the Soiree on the Bay construction. He'd need to be back on site first thing Monday morning for the final push on the project. It exhausted him to think about it, so he didn't, instead having a few margaritas and enjoying several hours out by the pool with Lexi, Angie, and his other guests. Now that the festivities were winding down and only a few people remained, it would've been easy to start worrying about work again. Luckily, he had Lexi to distract him.

"You throw quite a party," she said. It was just the two of them sitting under an umbrella in lounge chairs side by side.

Jack was enjoying the spectacular view of her in a bikini. This one was also black but a bit more modest than the other one. It didn't matter too much to him. He was content looking at her curves and the stretches of her bare skin. "I hope you've enjoyed yourself. I know it's been a lot. You've met a ton of people you didn't know." He would never say a word to Lexi, but he had worried about whether she would fit in at this party. Not only did she have to navigate conversation with his sister, which could be tricky in its own right, she had to make small talk with strangers, many of whom were tied to Bowden Construction. That was not Lexi's world. Just like banking was not his.

"You make everything fun." Lexi leaned over for a quick kiss. "Your sister and I actually chatted about that."

Jack had been wondering how he was going to find out what those two had talked about. He was glad Lexi had brought up the subject herself. "You care to share any other parts of your conversation?"

"It might sound horrible, but we sort of bonded over our divorces. It was nice to confide in someone else who has gone through it."

Jack was glad they'd found common ground. He knew that Angie could put up roadblocks and she would always be protective of Jack, just like he was protective of her. "That makes sense. You've both been through a hard time. I'm glad you were able to talk to her about it. You might have some helpful perspective for her. I think Angie still feels like her life has ended. I'm trying to remind her that she has lots of time to build a life."

Jack felt like that was solid advice, but he didn't necessarily think it pertained to him. He didn't have as much runway ahead of him as his sister. At thirty-nine, with his career well established, Jack was starting to think he should get serious. Funnily enough, Lexi was the person who'd made him doubt the very notion of keeping things casual when he'd been perfectly content with it for a long time. He understood why she wanted it that way—her personal history demanded it. But he also knew the other reason he'd gone along with it from the start. He'd worried they wouldn't get along. However, as it turned out, quite the opposite was true.

Angie wandered over. "I don't want to sound completely lame, but I think I'm going to head home. I'm beat."

"Are you okay to drive?" Jack asked.

"Rich is going to drive me. He hasn't had anything to drink. I'll come back tomorrow to get my car."

Jack got up from his seat to give his sister a hug. "I hope you had fun."

"I did, Jack. It was awesome." She patted him on the shoulder, then turned to Lexi. "It was great to meet you. Thank you for the bracelet. I love it." Angie held up her arm, showing off the very thoughtful gift Lexi had bought.

"Oh, good. I'm really glad you like it. It was nice to meet you, too," she said.

Angie pulled Jack aside. "Actually, can I steal a minute? Inside?"

"Yeah. Of course." He turned to Lexi. "I'm going to help Angie grab her stuff."

The pair made their way inside to the living room, where she'd opened her presents. They both sat on the couch, Angie loading up a gift bag with her birthday haul, while Jack gathered spent wrapping paper bound for the recycling.

"I want you to know that I like her. A lot. I

thought she was going to be a bubbleheaded rich girl, but she's not that at all. She's very thoughtful and down to earth."

Jack was fairly certain that was the case, but he was still relieved to hear it from his sister. "I'm really happy to hear that. Thank you."

"But there's one thing you need to realize."

Here we go. "Yeah. Of course. Tell me."

"Knowing the way I feel right now, she's still really hurting from her divorce. There will be some days when she's over the moon with you and others when she's not sure. I'm learning that it's part of the process. Your whole life gets shaken up, and it makes you question everything."

Jack nodded, solemnly, taking in the things his sister had said. "Keep taking it slow."

"Exactly."

"Okay. I appreciate you telling me that."

Angie got up from the couch and picked up her gift bag. "One more thing. She noticed that you didn't introduce you as her girlfriend. I think that's probably a conversation you should have."

"Was she upset? And how is that supposed to be part of taking it slow?" Jack felt more than a little overwhelmed by all of this.

Angie placed her hand on his forearm and shook her head. "She wasn't upset. In fact, she said she'd prefer that you be Jack and she'll be Lexi. So, I think you're good. But I also think you should probably talk about it."

"Got it." One thing Jack knew for sure was that Lexi had made serious inroads in his world today. If their romance was going to progress, he was going to have to find a way to fold himself into hers. That meant at some point he'd have to find common ground with Lexi's dad.

Angie kissed Jack on the cheek. "Thanks again for everything today. Now go spend some time with Lexi and I'll talk to you on Monday."

Jack watched as Angie found Rich in the kitchen and they turned down the central hall to leave. When Jack got back out to the pool, the final guests were heading out. "Thanks for coming."

"Thank you for a great day," they replied.

Jack joined Lexi under the umbrella again, sitting rather than reclining, and reached for her hand. A few minutes later, they were alone. That moment of recognition hit him every time this was the case—that he wanted her. Needed her. "Will you stay the night?" He stroked her fingers softly, but even that innocent touch had his body on high alert.

"I don't know if I can sleep over. Bianca dragged me to yoga this morning, so I made her promise me that she'd come over and help me go through the boxes in my garage. The only time she can get away from the kids is at 8:00 a.m."

"Ouch."

"I know. Right? Anyway, I want this move to a new house, once I find a place, to be a clean slate. There are a lot of memories of Houston and my marriage in those boxes. I think I'll feel better if I just get rid of all of it."

Jack was happy to hear that. Lexi was taking strides forward, and he saw that as an essential part of their future. "I'm happy to haul stuff away if you need it. I sure as heck have a big enough truck."

"That would be great. Can you come by tomorrow? Late afternoon or tomorrow night?"

"Sure thing." Jack decided then and there that if Winston was on the family compound tomorrow, he would talk to him. It wouldn't be a showdown, but rather he would try to patch things up.

"What else do you have going on tomorrow?"

"It's my only day off, so I'm definitely sleeping in. It'll be my last chance to catch up on some z's before I head back to Appaloosa."

Lexi smiled at him wistfully. "I can't wait until I can go back there."

"I'd suggest next weekend, but since we're supposed to finish up this week, I think I'm going to want a break from the island for a while."

"Perfectly understandable."

Jack lifted her hand to his lips. "But I promise we'll go back for another sexy escape."

Lexi climbed off her chair and stepped over to him. The sun was setting behind her, casting her beautiful body in a soft glow. "I think we can have our own sexy escape right here. It's early. I can stay for at least a few hours."

"That is music to my ears."

Ten

Jack was on his way to Lexi's late Sunday afternoon when his phone rang. It was Angie. He pressed the button on his in-dash display to answer the call.

"Hey. What's up?" he asked.

"I'm catching up on bookkeeping. The last check we got from the Soiree on the Bay festival bounced."

Jack was confounded. That had never happened before. "Seriously?"

"Yes. And it was presented at the bank twice."

"What was the amount?"

"Two-fifty."

Jack knew that his sister meant hundreds of thousands. A quarter of a million bucks. Still, he wasn't worried. Rusty Edmond would make it right. "Okay. I'll give Rusty a call."

"You on your way to Lexi's?"

Jack pulled up to the Pine Valley security gate and slowed down, but the guard waved him right through. Apparently, he'd been here quite a lot. "I am. Why are you asking with that tone?"

"No reason. Just thinking about how taking things slow means not seeing someone all the time."

A grumble left his throat. "It's our last chance to see each other before I have to finish up on Appaloosa. And I'm helping her get rid of some boxes. It's not exactly a romantic visit."

"Something tells me you'll make it romantic."

"I'm not having this discussion with you." Jack really hated how much his sister was capable of making sense and driving him crazy at the same time. "I need to call Rusty, okay?"

"Sure thing. I love you, Jack. That's the only reason I'm saying any of this. I like Lexi and I'd like to keep it that way. If she breaks your heart, or vice versa, it'll be bad for everyone."

"I'll keep all of that in mind. Goodbye, Angie." Jack ended the call and dialed Rusty's number. He was almost to Lexi's house and wasn't sure how long this call would take, so he pulled up to the curb in front of the Alderidge estate.

"Jack. This is a surprise," Rusty said when he answered.

"I know. I'm sorry if this is out of the blue and I'm sorry if it's an odd time to call."

"What can I do for you?" he asked, cutting right to the chase.

"I'm calling because the last check we got from the festival board didn't clear the bank."

"That must be a mistake."

"We sent it through twice. Maybe an accounting mix-up?"

"I sure as hell hope not. I never want to hear about people not getting paid, especially someone who's working as hard as you are."

"What you would like me to do? It's a quarter of a million dollars."

"I'll cut you a check myself. I'll talk to Billy and get it straightened out on our end. I'll have a courier bring it to your office first thing tomorrow morning."

"Sounds great. Thank you, Rusty, for taking care of this for me."

"I trust you're going to be at the cocktail party to celebrate the completion of the construction?"

As if he needed more pressure on him, Rusty had scheduled a postconstruction event for Wednesday night. That meant Jack *had* to hit the deadline. "As long as we finish on time, I'll be there. I might show up in work boots, but hopefully you'll still let me in the door."

Rusty managed a quiet laugh. "Bring a date. Lexi Alderidge if that's still going on."

"I'll see what I can do."

"I look forward to construction wrapping up so I can put a drink in your hand on Wednesday night."

That was only a few days away, but it seemed like a lifetime. Jack had so much work to do before then. So many things to accomplish. "Thanks, Rusty. I'll talk to you soon."

Jack ended the call and pulled up to the Alderidge's personal gate and entered the code. The light flashed red at him, so he punched it in again. "Dammit," he muttered to himself, calling Lexi's cell. Before she had a chance to answer, the gate rolled open. Jack ended the call, looking for Lexi on the other side of the entrance. But when he drove into their driveway, he saw Winston Alderidge standing there.

Okay then. I guess we're doing this right now. He put the car in Park and climbed out. Lexi was running down the driveway from her house. Jack really wished she wouldn't interfere. He wanted to have this conversation with Winston one-on-one.

"Mr. Alderidge." He extended his hand. "I'm sorry you had to open the gate for me. I couldn't get the code to work."

"The visitor codes automatically change every two weeks." To his credit, Winston *did* shake Jack's hand. Still, it wasn't a warm greeting.

Lexi arrived, breathless, barefoot and wearing one of her many dresses. "I wasn't thinking. The codes changed over."

Jack smiled at her. "It's no problem. If it's okay, I'd like to speak to your dad for a few minutes."

Lexi looked back and forth between him and her dad. Surely she sensed the tension between them. All the more reason to excuse herself. "Okay. I'll be home whenever you want to come over. I'm just going through some boxes." She took a few more steps over to him, popped up on to her tiptoes and went to kiss his cheek, but Jack had to lean down to let her do it. He appreciated the sentiment, and he had to admit it made him happy that she was willing to do that in front of her father.

With that, Lexi walked back down the driveway.

"Would you like to come in?" Winston asked.

"Really?" Jack didn't want to sound so surprised, but he was. "I mean, yes. Thank you."

"For a minute. My daughter doesn't like to wait for anyone or anything, but I'd also rather not have this conversation in the driveway."

"Perfectly understandable." He trailed behind Winston, filled with trepidation, but also a tiny glimmer of hope. Surely the man wouldn't invite him in just to yell at him.

When they walked inside, it occurred to Jack that this was a glimpse into Lexi's life that he hadn't been privy to before. This was the original ivory tower his favorite princess had grown up in. It was pure luxury, of course, with an added edge of stuffiness that came as no surprise. There were formal settees in the marble-floored foyer and crystal chandeliers overhead. Winston led Jack down a long hallway lined with dark wallpaper and dozens of family portraits. He caught a glimpse of one of Lexi as a teenager and had to pause to look. She had a mouth full of metal.

Winston stopped and laughed when he saw the picture Jack was looking at. "She hated those braces. Couldn't wait for them to come off."

Jack was a bit shell-shocked. He hadn't known Winston was capable of expressing humor. "She's still cute." Jack dared to make direct eye contact with the older man, and it felt as though they had an entire conversation, acknowledging that Winston loved his daughter deeply and would protect her at any cost, and that Jack was her unwavering admirer who would not back down, even when faced with her dad's wrath.

"Indeed." Winston continued down the hall, and through a door at the very end.

Jack stepped into Winston's study. It practically looked like a museum dedicated to Alderidge family history in Royal. The walls were covered with framed awards and photos of the man with local dignitaries, the shelves lined with golf trophies. As he took survey of it all, he realized that perhaps the reason Winston was so stuck in Royal was because he'd been immersed in it for so long. That wasn't necessarily a bad thing. Jack had once felt that way about San Antonio and his circle of friends there. Hell, he'd dragged Rich and his sister here just so he could feel connected to someone and something. Although he didn't agree with snobbery, especially when it came to money, he might be understanding Winston a bit better.

"You play golf, Jack?" Winston asked.

"I've done it a few times, sir, but it's not really my forte. I enjoy other sports, though. I play a lot of one-on-one basketball with my best friend. Laps in the pool. Things like that."

"I see. Well, if you ever decide to try your hand at it, let me know. I'll gladly take you out."

Jack appreciated the offer, but he was skeptical of what was going on here. "Can I ask why the change of heart, sir? That moment we met at the TCC, you looked like you were ready to skin me alive, and all I'd done was dance with your daughter. I know for a fact that I wasn't the first man to do that, so I couldn't help but think that I was the *wrong* one."

Winston leaned back against the edge of his sizable mahogany desk and folded his arms over his chest. Jack couldn't help but notice that through the windows directly behind Lexi's, there was a perfect view of her cottage, especially the front door, where Jack had kissed her after their first date. That couldn't have helped his case that night at the TCC. "I like you, Jack."

"You'd better be sure about that, because if it's the truth, I'm going to hold you to it."

Winston quirked an eyebrow and nodded. "See? Right there. That's what I like. You're direct. You don't beat around the bush."

"I don't see the point."

"Neither do I." He cleared his throat then went on to say, "I wanted you to know that I went back and looked at the loan application you submitted all those years ago. The source of the rift between us."

"And?"

"In my defense, you hadn't been in business in Royal for very long."

"Seven plus years had been more than enough time to get myself established," Jack informed him. "I was turning down work at that time, which is why I needed the capital to expand."

"I understand. But there's something about Royal. It's a wonderful place to live, but it takes time to get in deep and gain people's trust. And this is where I get to the part where I admit to my mistake, which was that I didn't know you or your company at that point, and so I assumed you were a fly-by-night operation. I hadn't given the numbers a close enough look. Your projections were solid and I should have granted the loan. I apologize."

"If I can be frank, it was more than the rejection, sir. It was your tone. It sent a pretty clear message that I was not only not part of the inner circles of Royal, but that I might never be." Jack realized his retort had been bottled up for a long time.

Winston nodded. "I know. And I'm sorry for that, as well. Lexi and I have had many conversations about exactly that since she's come to work at the bank. You know, when you're the boss, and you've been doing your job for a long time, you don't always stop to think about the ways you present yourself." He hesitated for a moment, then confided, "Business is going great and you assume that everyone loves you and wants to work with you. But I've been learning from Lexi that I might catch a few more flies with honey than with vinegar."

Funny, but Angie had accused Jack of being grumpy in the office just the other day. "I understand. I'm glad Lexi has shown you a different way to do business."

"I was reluctant to step into the future because the history of our bank is one of our biggest selling points. People want a financial institution that's been around for a long time. But they also want one that's pleasant to work with. I need to remember that."

Jack felt the need to bring up the elephant in the

room—Lexi. "I care about your daughter deeply." His voice cracked at the end of his sentence, emotion welling up inside him.

"I understand that. And I believe she cares about you, too."

"Does that mean things are square between us?" Jack asked.

"More or less. I mean, I am still her father, and I will fight you to the death if you dare to hurt her."

"Good to know."

The older man looked him square in the eye. "Tread lightly, Jack. The girl has been through the wringer."

So he'd been told. "I will, sir. I promise." Jack reached over to shake Winston's hand one more time. "I'd better go. I'm sure Lexi is wondering what we're talking about."

"Oh, I guarantee she's dying to know."

Lexi was supposed to be going through the boxes she'd brought in from the garage, but she kept pulling back her living room curtains, trying to deduce what was going on in her dad's study. He and Jack were definitely in there. What were they talking about? Were they having another argument? Lexi really hoped not because she didn't want to have to do damage control. She'd said her piece to her dad. He needed to get with the program.

Maybe it's for the best, she thought to herself, although just as fast, she banished it from her brain. She didn't want to walk away from Jack. The problem was that she felt like circumstances were pushing them in that direction of serious—the weekend away, the pool party, the phone sex… Jack had opened up her whole world, and she wasn't ready for that to end. But every shared experience they had brought them closer to what Lexi was rightfully scared of—commitment.

Lexi took another peek outside, and Jack was headed up the sidewalk in front of her house. She let go of the curtain and allowed it to fall back into place, then rushed to the door. "What happened?"

Jack came to a dead stop and his killer smile crossed his lips. Every time he did that, her fears evaporated, even if it was only for a few seconds. She adored him. She wanted him. And against all odds, wanted things to work between them. "Were you worried?"

"Of course I was. Have you *met* me?" She stood back to let him in, then closed the door behind him. "How could I not worry? I know my dad and I know you, and never the twain shall meet."

"Actually, we had a good conversation. He apologized."

Lexi felt like she might need to have her ears cleaned out. Was this a trick? "You're not serious. I've never heard him say he was sorry. About anything."

Jack ventured into her great room and took a seat at the end of one of the couches. He patted the empty spot next to him. "Come here, beautiful. I'll tell you everything."

Lexi eagerly took the invitation, settling in on the cushion and immediately leaning into Jack's firm, solid frame as he put his arm around her. "So it was good?"

"It wasn't perfect, but I think we understand each other. He said he was sorry about the loan, and he explained that he has a blind spot for the established Royal businesses and families. He actually admitted you've been a big part of convincing him that he needs to open his eyes to everything around him."

She still found it hard to believe what Jack was saying. "I feel like I'm drilling that into his head all day long. There is so much business available in Royal, and we could do such a better job being a part of the community. He's just so stuck in his ways."

"Or, as he sees it, he's loyal to the town where he's raised a family and lived his whole life," Jack said. "There's nothing wrong with remembering where you come from and the people who helped you get where you are today. That's important to me, too."

"Like Angie and Rich."

"Yes. Exactly."

It occurred to her that they'd each basically gotten the stamp of approval from their respective loved ones. That left only Lexi's muddled brain as she tried to figure out of what she was truly ready for with Jack. "So, what else did he have to say?"

"He said I need to tread lightly when it comes to you. And that he'd hunt me down and kill me if I ever hurt you."

"You have nothing to worry about. I can't imagine you ever hurting me." Lexi feared it was the other way around. She didn't question Jack's feelings about her, even though neither of them had put it into words beyond saying that they liked each other and had a lot of fun together. But she was in zero rush to get to big important labels. She knew the way he made her feel—like she was cherished. That she mattered. That her thoughts and feelings were real and she was entitled to process them in her own time.

But she also wasn't stupid. She'd seen the way other women looked at him—at Sheen, at the TCC, and even at his own pool party. She also knew that once a woman got to know Jack the way Lexi knew him, she likely wouldn't ever let him go. Angie had said that he'd spent years not taking relationships seriously, all because he'd had his heart broken more than a decade ago. Didn't it reason that at some point, Jack would decide he wanted to settle down? He was almost forty. Would he wait around for her to get over her hang-ups, or would he grow impatient and want to move on?

"I'm glad you have confidence in me." Jack took her hand and they twined their fingers together. It was a bit comical the way his were so much bigger than hers, the way they almost threatened to swallow hers up, but however funny, it was also the perfect illustration of them as a pair. They were very different people, who somehow worked together.

"I knew from the moment I met you that you were a man of your word."

"That's not true. I was giving you a hard time and not being entirely truthful about who I was or what I was doing."

"Okay. That's fair." She playfully swatted his leg with her one free hand. "But that's also the day you came to my rescue. And I'm very grateful that you did. If you hadn't, we never would've gotten to know each other." Lexi was suddenly hit with a vision of what would've happened if Jack hadn't acted that day, or even worse, if she hadn't accepted his invitation. She would've missed out on so much—which added up to a lot more than hot nights and unbridled passion. There had been laughter, contentment and tenderness, too.

"One of the smartest things I ever did." He leaned over and kissed her temple. "I will give you all the time you need, Lexi. Your dad asked that of me, and I intend to do that. I'm happy with the way things are right now. But I also need you to know that you do mean something to me. This isn't just a fling for me."

Lexi's heart started to hammer. She'd just been thinking about how she didn't need words. "Yes. I'm happy with the way things are right now, too. I have a lot of changes ahead. Finding a house. Moving. I'm still figuring out my job. I like that we've kept things casual and fun."

Jack cleared his throat. "It's definitely been fun. That's for sure."

She wondered if she'd said the wrong thing, but decided her truth was always right. That was what Jack would want from her. "I hate to say this, but I should probably finish going through these last two boxes. You can relax and we can talk while I work."

"I thought I was here to be the muscle."

Lexi laughed, appreciating that the mood had been lightened a bit. She patted his thigh before getting to her feet, then reached down for his hand in an effort to pull him off the couch. "Fine, Muscle Man. I'll show you which boxes can go in the truck."

Jack feigned a scowl but rose out of his seat. Lexi walked across the room to the stack of boxes filled with things she wanted to get rid of. He came up behind her and placed his hands on her hips, leaning down and snuggling her neck with soft kisses.

"Jack. This doesn't feel like lifting boxes. This feels like something else."

He pressed against her backside. "How does *this* feel?"

She giggled, but it came out more like a moan. He didn't have to work very hard to make her want him. "It feels like you're wanting to go in the other room."

"Or here. I'm up for whatever you want." He brushed her hair to one side and kissed her neck while he gathered the hem of her dress in his hand then palmed the upper part of her bare thigh, his fingers dangerously close to her center.

A gasp left Lexi's lips as she rolled her head to one side to let him take full purchase of her skin. "I just want you, Jack. That's as much brain power as I can put into it right now."

Jack needed no further invitation. He took charge like he always did, scooping her up in his arms and carrying her off to her bedroom. "I've been in your dad's office. I know what a good view he has of your house. At least things are private back here."

"Smart man."

Jack set her feet on the floor then lifted her dress over her head and unhooked her bra. He sat on the edge of her bed and she stood between his legs. Their eyes met and held. Then he bent down, taking her nipple between his lips, sucking and rolling his tongue over the firm bud. All of Lexi's blood left her head, aiming straight at her center, which was now ablaze with desire for him. She removed his shirt, then he wriggled her panties past her hips.

Lexi climbed up on the bed, straddling his lap. He reclined back on the mattress while slipping his hand between her legs and caressing her most delicate spot. The rough denim of his jeans rubbed against the tender skin of her inner thighs, but she loved the contrast between the sensations. Like every other time he'd touched her, it felt impossibly good, but it was like he automatically knew now exactly what she liked. He paid attention. He…cared.

"We need to get you out of these jeans." Lexi shifted from his lap and rummaged through her bedside table drawer for a condom.

Jack stood and shucked his pants, then took the foil packet from her and rolled on the condom. Lexi was about to stretch out on the bed, but he surprised her and picked her up again. Pressing her back against the wall, he wrapped one of her legs around his hip and she followed suit with the other. She had never done it in this position, but then again, she'd never been with a guy as strong as Jack. He drove inside and she pulled him closer, with her ankles crossed and her heels pressing on his backside. His kisses came hot and wet, and the pressure built impossibly fast, even more so than the other times they'd made love.

Jack was taking hard, fast thrusts, forcing her

hips into the wall, and ragged breaths from her lips. She was already at the edge of her peak. Hovering. Reaching. So close. But not yet. Lexi let her mind go and focused on his kiss, the touch of his skin against hers, and how she could be totally uninhibited with him without worry. She trusted him. Implicitly.

When her body gave way, she burrowed her face in his neck, biting down on his skin while the stubble along his jaw dug into her cheek. She called out against his skin and Jack did, too, only he wasn't quite so quiet. His body convulsed and neither said anything, arms wrapped tightly around each other, both of them struggling for breaths.

Jack gently set her down and stepped into her bathroom to dispose of the condom. When he walked back into her room, Lexi was sprawled on the bed. He happily stretched out next to her.

"That was unbelievable," she said, rolling to her side and placing her hand on his chest.

"Really? It seemed totally believable to me. We work well together."

Jack had an excellent point. Their chemistry was so electric that this part of their relationship was undeniably perfect. The rest of it was great, too, for that matter. "Are you thirsty? Hungry? Can I get you anything?"

"I'd love a glass of water for now." Jack scooted

back on the bed, then pulled back half of the duvet and climbed underneath it.

"I'll be right back." Lexi grabbed her silk robe from the closet and wrapped herself in it before padding off to the kitchen. She stood at the fridge, filling two glasses from the water dispenser. Through the kitchen window, she could see the lights on in her parents' house. She still couldn't really believe Jack had made peace with her dad. It was remarkable.

Glasses filled, Lexi also grabbed a package of chocolate sandwich cookies from the pantry to deliver it all to the bedroom. But the instant she walked through the door, she saw the loveliest sight. "Aww. He fell asleep." Jack had turned onto his side, tucked one arm under the pillow and was deep in a peaceful slumber. His eyes were closed, his mouth slack. She set down the glasses of water, perched lightly on the edge of her bed and took out a cookie, nibbling on it as she watched him sleep. Jack had never slept over at her place before, and Lexi knew for a fact that her dad was aware that he was there. Heck, his truck was still in the driveway. But Jack had been working so hard, she couldn't bear to wake him.

She went into her bathroom to brush her teeth and wash her face, then turned off the lights and climbed into bed next to him. It wasn't easy to snuggle with Jack—he was so big. But she could mold her body next to his, and that was what she did. Her only thought as she drifted off to sleep was that she was in big trouble. Not so much with her dad, but with her own heart.

Eleven

Waking up in Lexi's bed shortly before five in the morning was the worst possible start to Jack's week. He stumbled around in the dark, searching for his clothes in the somewhat unfamiliar landscape of Lexi's bedroom, trying not to wake her. When he stubbed his toe on her dresser, he failed.

"Ouch!" He did his best to swallow back his outburst as he hopped around the room on one foot.

"Jack?" Lexi's sleepy voice sounded as disoriented as he felt.

"I'm so sorry I woke you. I'm trying to get my clothes so I can get out of here. I'm going to be late. I'm supposed to meet Rich at the landing strip at six."

Lexi switched on the small lamp on her bedside table, blinking as she got used to the sudden burst of light. "I'm sorry."

Jack grabbed his remaining clothes to finish getting dressed. "You should have woken me last night. My car is out in the driveway…which means your dad knows I slept over. I told him I'd take things slow, and then I do this?"

Lexi laughed quietly. "I'm pretty sure he knows we're having sex, Jack."

"It's not funny. He probably does, but it's the principle of the thing. I want him to know I'm an upstanding guy. This is not what an upstanding guy does."

"It's no big deal. So, you fell asleep. You're exhausted, which is no surprise. You're working like crazy."

Jack drew in a deep breath, trying to clear his head and calm down. He didn't want to blow things with Lexi, and that included messing things up with her dad. "I'm sorry. I guess I'm stressed. The next three days are going to be a nightmare."

Lexi climbed out of bed and grabbed her robe, which was draped over the back of a chair. "I know. And I'm sorry. But try to focus on the big party at Rusty's Wednesday night. You'll be done then." She gently placed her hand on his arm, peering up at him.

As soon as she touched him, he felt a bit better. "You're right. I just need to get through this final push."

"You'll do great."

"Thanks. I should get going." Jack made sure he had his keys and wallet, then walked out into Lexi's living room with her trailing behind him. "Oh, damn. I can't take these boxes for you right now. Can I do it this weekend?"

"Yes. Of course. Don't worry about it."

Jack felt like he was letting everyone down. "I'm sorry. That was the whole reason I came over in the first place."

"Last night was great, Jack. You talked things out with my dad. We got to have some superhot sex. Try to look on the bright side. The boxes can wait."

She was right. Of course. "Thank you for being so amazing."

"Anytime. Now get going." She shooed him toward the door. "Call me if you have a spare minute over the next few days?"

"I'll make time." He pulled her into his arms and kissed her, knowing this blip of time with Lexi would have to fuel him for the next few days. "Talk to you soon."

Jack walked double-time to his car, being very careful to close his door quietly. Moments later, he zipped out the security gate and through Pine Valley, racing home to grab his bags, then turning around to get to the airstrip. Rich and the pilot were

waiting for him, but he was only about fifteen minutes late. It could've been worse.

"You okay?" Rich asked as they both buckled in.

"Yeah. Fine. Just preoccupied with the job." In
truth, it was more than that. There was this emp-
tiness inside him that refused to go away. He felt
unsettled. Off his game. The two things he wanted
most felt just out of reach—finishing this job and
getting Lexi to take the idea of them as a couple
more seriously. All he could do was forge ahead. Do
his best. Let things play out as they would.

"You and me both," Rich said. "You and me
both."

As per usual, construction wrapped up with zero
time to spare, and it wasn't 100 percent done. There
were still a few tiny details to finish, but Rusty had
been insistent that they proclaim the project complete. He'd invited a heap of people to the Edmond
estate for the celebratory cocktail party, and he said
it would've been an embarrassment to postpone.
And, despite his trepidation, Jack saw where the
old man was coming from. Delaying the shindig
would most assuredly cast a pall over the excitement surrounding the Soiree on the Bay project. But
the worst part about being late was that he'd had to
ask Lexi to meet him at the party. Once again, he
felt like he was falling short.

Jack called her as he approached the security

gate on the perimeter of the Edmond estate. Ahead, a long line of cars trailed up the driveway, brake lights glowing red against a darkening night sky. Surrounded by miles of pristine ranch land, the property featured a pool, stables and several guest-houses. It was notorious in Royal, one of the largest private tracts within the county limits. Currently a bachelor, Rusty lived here with his daughter, Gina, and stepson Asher. Soiree on the Bay mastermind Billy Holmes also resided on the grounds, currently occupying one of the guest cottages.

"Are you stuck in this traffic jam outside the house?" Jack asked.

"I just parked," Lexi answered. "I'll wait for you outside."

"Perfect. Thanks." Jack drummed his thumbs on the steering wheel, feeling impatient. All he wanted was to see Lexi, have a drink and find somewhere to sit down. Attending a cocktail party was quite literally the last thing he wanted to do right now, but he'd make the best of it.

"It just occurred to me—I don't think I've been to Rusty's since I was a teenager," Lexi said.

"It's been a few months for me. Rusty sometimes invites me to his poker parties."

"I'm surprised you never ran into my dad here," she remarked. "He's not much of a card player, but he loves to smoke cigars with Rusty so he'll some-times come for one for those games."

"I don't always accept the invitation. Mostly because I don't enjoy losing thousands of dollars in one night the way Rusty does. I'd rather hold on to my money. I guess you could say that old habits die hard." As soon as the words came out of his mouth, he realized that he had one old habit he was eager to cast aside—his penchant for keeping things casual with a woman forever. He'd spent a lot of time thinking over the last three days, imagining what came next for Lexi and him—months of casual dating, long, passionate nights, and a lot of back and forth between their two houses, no matter where she ended up living. He loved what they had together, but there was a voice in his head saying it wasn't enough.

"These cars are not moving fast," Lexi lamented.

"Rusty told me the guest list is huge."

"Are you nervous?" she asked as he got closer to the massive house, which was all lit up in dramatic fashion.

It wasn't nerves he was feeling. "No. I need a nap though. I'm definitely sleeping in this weekend."

"I know you're exhausted. It was so adorable the way you fell asleep the other night at my place."

"Don't remind me," he grumbled. "I'm still unhappy about that."

"Pretty soon, we won't have to worry about it at all. I'll be at my new place."

It made Jack feel a bit better to hear her say "we"

along with mention of future plans, but as he got closer to the house and he saw the news van parked out front, his stomach sank. "Oh, crap. The *Royal Tonight!* van is here. That means Mandee Meriweather is going to be there. She's so nosy."

"Seriously. I spoke with her a week or so ago, to tell her about the bank's involvement with Soiree on the Bay, but all she wanted to focus on was you and me."

"You didn't tell me that."

"I guess I forgot."

Finally, the cars were moving ahead. Jack was directed into a parking space in the expansive stone driveway in front of the house. "I'm going to do my best to avoid her. She's given me a hard time in the past, and has this deluded idea that I'm a playboy. Which is utterly ridiculous."

"From everything I've heard it's the truth."

Jack knew that Angie had run her mouth about how many women he had dated. But he didn't want Lexi thinking about that. Ever. "Whatever my sister told you, I'm positive she embellished. She does that."

"Last time I checked, you were happy that your sister and I get along."

He drew in a deep breath. "I am happy about that." He climbed out of his car and clicked his fob to lock the doors. "Where are you?"

Lexi laughed, but the sound wasn't coming only from his phone. "Right behind you."

Jack turned around, confronted by the beautiful sight before him. She was absolutely gorgeous, in a sparkly black dress that made her red hair flame. He couldn't help but gather her up in his arms, spin her around. His whole body felt lighter, just from seeing her. Her kiss was sweet and familiar. Perfect.

"You seem really tense, Jack," she said when he put her back down on the ground.

If only she knew that seeing her made any tension go away. "I'm just tired."

"Let's get you inside and get you a drink. Hopefully that will reenergize you."

"First, I need to tell you that you look absolutely stunning tonight." The words felt so inadequate. She was more than beautiful and sexy. She was everything he'd never known he wanted.

"And *you* look incredibly handsome. But, then again, you always do." She spread her hand across the lapel of his charcoal gray suit.

Jack smiled at the praise. Having her look at him like that was like being under the gaze of an angel. "Thank you." He leaned down and kissed her cheek. "I love having you with me tonight."

Lexi beamed up at him. "I love that you asked me."

A sigh left his lips as he took her hand and they walked up to the wide steps leading up to the Edmond home. Although he appreciated every sweet thing she said, he wanted more. He could admit that to himself. The question was when he could feel good about admitting it to her.

As soon as Lexi and Jack stepped over the threshold of the Edmond home and were greeted by Rusty, she started to feel on edge. She loved Royal, but the pressure in these old money circles, where people came to a party to see and be seen, weighed on her. There was so much judgment and appraisal in the air, everyone trying to outdo each other, and stake their claim in the social pecking order. She may have grown up in this sort of environment, and she may have even thrived in it at times, but in the aftermath of being left at the altar, Lexi had truly learned just how empty and ruthless the trappings of wealth and power could be.

"Jack!" Rusty exclaimed, clapping him on the shoulder. "You're the man of the hour. I'm so glad you're here. There are so many people wanting to talk to you tonight. Including some other investors you should have a chat with. I'd also like you to talk to Mandee Meriweather from *Royal Tonight!* She's doing a big story on the festival. We've got to light a fire under the PR machine."

Jack pulled Lexi closer to his side. "If it's all the same to you, Rusty, I'd like to first focus on getting Lexi and myself a drink. We both could use it."

The tycoon smiled. "Oh, yes. Of course. Please help yourselves. I'll hunt you down in a little bit."

Lexi couldn't help but notice that Rusty had hardly acknowledged her. There had been a time when that really would've irked her, but she could let it go now. That was really progress for her. "What do you want to drink?" she asked Jack as they approached the bar.

"Rusty always has the best of the best, so I'll definitely go for a bourbon. What do you want, sweetheart?"

Lexi was about to tell Jack that she wanted champagne, but she first had to address something else. *"Sweetheart?"*

"What?" Confusion clouded his expression. "Does it bother you that I called you that?"

Lexi enjoyed the expression of affection, but he'd made an unfortunate choice. "I think it's sweet that you want to call me that, but that's the endearment Roger used for me. So, it doesn't feel great to hear it."

Jack's face immediately fell. "I'm so sorry. I didn't know."

"You couldn't have. It's okay. It was still such a sweet thing to say." She hated the thought of hurting Jack's feelings.

"I'll think of something better, okay?"

Lexi pulled him closer as they stepped up to the bar. "Perfect."

Jack ordered their drinks, and they walked over to a relatively quiet corner. The room was packed with people milling around, conversation and music steadily gaining volume. "I don't know how much of this I can take," Jack said.

"But you're the man of the hour."

"That's just an excuse for Rusty to hype the festival."

"Or maybe he sincerely wants to celebrate your accomplishment." Lexi was about to share more encouragement when she saw a bright light out of the corner of her eye. Making her way through the crowd was Mandee Meriweather and a cameraman from *Royal Tonight!*

"Jack Bowden!" Mandee exclaimed, wagging a finger at him. "You've been hiding from me."

"I haven't. Just got here."

"Well, I need an interview with you right now. We *have* to discuss Soiree on the Bay."

Jack didn't seem happy about it but agreed. "Sure. Okay."

Mandee glanced at Lexi. "Hey, Lexi. Do you mind moving out of the shot?"

She had to swallow back how insulted she felt by the request. It hadn't been that long ago that Mandee was eager to interview her, but she reminded herself that tonight was Jack's night. Lexi was here for support. "Gladly."

Mandee cozied up to Jack and Lexi slugged back

her champagne, hoping it would help to tamp down her jealousy. The reporter exchanged words with the cameraman, just as Rusty arrived to watch. Jack became noticeably more tense. Lexi's heart really went out to him. She knew how much he did not enjoy being the center of attention.

Mandee looked directly into the camera. "Mandee Meriweather here, broadcasting live from the lavish Edmond estate. Tonight is the scene of a grand cocktail party, where the Royal elite are gathered to honor Jack Bowden, whose company just completed construction on the Soiree on the Bay festival site on Appaloosa Island."

Mandee smiled widely, then turned her attention to Jack, asking about the upcoming festival and the hoops he and his crews had jumped through to get the construction completed on time. Jack provided succinct answers, thinly veiling his annoyance that he had to endure this at all.

"Now, Jack—" Mandee planted her hand on his shoulder "—the last time we talked, you were single. Since then, lots of folks in Royal have spotted you and Lexi Alderidge together, but when I recently asked her about you, she said that you were just friends. She was adamant that you were nothing more."

Lexi felt as though her stomach had just dropped to her knees. She had given that answer to protect Jack and her. And certainly hadn't meant it the way Mandee made it sound. Lexi stepped closer to the cameraman, trying to catch Jack's attention. When their gazes connected, the disappointment on his face was so profound, it was a dagger plunged straight through her heart. All she could do was mouth, *I'm sorry.*

Jack cleared his throat, then directed his attention to Mandee. "Yes. That's true. Lexi and I are friends. That's it."

Mandee unleashed a sly grin that made Lexi nauseous. She turned to the camera. "You heard it here first, ladies of Royal. Jack Bowden, the man behind the Soiree on the Bay construction, is single."

Jack waited for only a few more seconds before he asked, "Is that it?"

"I got everything I wanted," Mandee answered.

Jack stepped out from the bright camera light and took Lexi's hand. "We need to talk." As ominous as that sounded, she was eager to explain herself. Jack turned to Rusty. "Is there anyone in your study right now?"

Their host shook his head. "No. The door is closed."

"Perfect. Is it okay if I steal it for a few minutes?"

Rusty seemed utterly confused. "Is everything okay, Jack?"

Jack's grip on Lexi's hand loosened ever so slightly, but it felt like he was sending her a message about exactly how unhappy he was. "Everything's perfect. Lexi and I just need to have a chat."

"Don't be long. I have a lot of people I want you to speak with tonight."

"Got it." With Lexi in tow, Jack stalked through the door on the far side of the room and down a quiet hall. He seemed to know exactly where he was going, opening Rusty's office and slipping inside.

"I'm sorry, Jack," Lexi blurted as soon as the door was closed.

"Did you mean it? That we're just friends and that's it?"

"Well, yes. I mean, what else would you have wanted me to say to her? You hate gossip just as much as I do. Did you actually want me to tell her that we were involved?"

He stared down at her, a muscle ticking in his jaw. "I would've hoped that you would tell her the truth. I don't have a lot of patience for skirting that."

Lexi could hardly believe what he was saying. "Her whole job is twisting people's words to try and make them sound more exciting and salacious. I wasn't going to feed into that."

"I see your point. It still doesn't mean it isn't disappointing." Jack shook his head and paced to the other side of the room. "Or frustrating. Or slowly driving me crazy."

Lexi felt as though she was completely out of her

depth. "Frustrating you how? I don't understand what you're trying to say."

He came to a stop and looked her square in the eye. "I love you, Lexi. I love you and it hurts like hell to know that you aren't where I am. It hurts to know that I've finally found the person I want to be with and she's not sure."

Lexi needed a minute to absorb the things he'd just said. The thing was, the idea of love wasn't as outlandish as the reason why she couldn't bear to hear him say it. "I—I don't know what to say."

"You don't feel like I do. I get it. I don't want you to tell me something you don't feel." He turned to the window and hung his head. "And now I feel like a jerk for putting you on the spot."

"It's not that, Jack. Don't feel bad. I don't want that."

"Then what *do* you want, Lexi?"

There was something so simple and yet so devastating about that question. Part of her wanted to go back, to a time when she hadn't been hurt so badly. When she was the old Lexi who took things in stride and had very few troubles. And yet, she knew that she couldn't go back. She knew it as well as her own name. "I want those three words to not hurt so much."

He turned back to her, betrayal blazing in his eyes. "How could it hurt to hear that I love you? You spend so much time questioning the way people feel about you, the way they see you." He stepped closer, his physical presence overwhelming her senses. "And I'm telling you that I look at you and all I know is that I want to see you every day. All I know is that you make me happier than I've ever been."

"Jack. We've known each other for a month."

He froze and his eyes glistened with emotion. "I know. That's what's so scary. I feel like this after a month. Doesn't that mean that what's between us will just grow into more?"

Lexi wished she could feel so optimistic about the future. Now she really did want to go back—to a mere hour ago, when the genie hadn't yet been let out of the bottle and he'd said those three little words. "Do you want to know why it hurts when you tell me that you love me?"

"Yes. I need to know. Because it doesn't make any sense to me."

"Because the other two men who said those words to me didn't mean it." She heard her voice cracking and wobbling. "I built my life around two people who told me they loved me, but ultimately didn't. And the thought of one more person saying it and later changing their mind? I can't live through that, Jack. Not again."

"I'm not going to change my mind, Lexi."

"You don't know that. They did."

He sucked in a deep breath. He'd never seemed

more exasperated. "I don't know what I can do to convince you. And whatever it is, I don't see a way I'm supposed to persuade you in five minutes when we're standing in Rusty Edmond's study."

"What are you saying, Jack? Are you saying you don't want to see me anymore?"

He pressed his lips together firmly. "I don't think I can move forward if we aren't on the same page. I'm a patient man, Lexi, but there's a limit to that. I think we need to take a break. You need to spend some time thinking and I need to do the same."

Lexi choked back her tears, mindlessly nodding, even when she didn't agree with what he was saying. A break was stupid. It meant breaking up, when she'd felt like they were only getting started. "Okay, then. I'm going to go home."

"You don't have to go. Stay. Have fun." Jack reached for her hand, but Lexi stepped back and headed for the door. It was only going to hurt to touch him. It was just going to break her heart.

"You know as well as I do that there's nothing fun about this."

Twelve

Lexi couldn't sleep after the cocktail party at the Edmond estate. Her bed felt cold and lonely, but it also felt like what she deserved. Everything that had happened last night tumbled through her head like a boulder rolling down a hill—building speed and gaining momentum. The faster her thoughts traveled, the worse they seemed to get.

She couldn't escape the sense that she'd made a huge mistake by telling Jack that it hurt to hear "I love you." It was the truth, but it wasn't the *whole* truth. It wasn't Jack. It wasn't the words. It was the echoes of the pain they'd created. They wouldn't stop reverberating through her head. Through her body. She had to stop giving her history so much power over her. But she didn't know how to do that. Meanwhile, a once-in-a-lifetime man might be slipping away.

A little after 4:00 a.m., she'd had enough of tossing and turning, and decided she had to do something. Going through the final box from Houston seemed like the most obvious choice. If she was going to keep her past from ruining her future, she wanted to discard the remaining physical vestiges of it.

Lexi turned on the overhead light in the living room and walked over to the corner where the boxes sat. She picked up the one unopened carton and lugged it over to her coffee table, cutting the packing tape with a pair of scissors. When she pulled the flaps open, she found a smaller box inside. She already knew what was in there. Lots and lots of old photos. Part of her wanted to simply set it aside for another time. Another day when she wasn't feeling quite so broken.

But no. It was time to do this. She tossed aside the lid and grabbed a stack of photos. They were candids of her and Roger with their friends at a bar. It was the night he'd proposed. Her first reaction was that her hair looked ridiculous. She wasn't sure what she'd been thinking. Her second thought was that she was wearing her fake smile in every picture. She knew that expression. It was the one that appeared when her parents dragged her to an event she didn't want to be at. It was the one she painted on her face when she knew everyone expected her to just be happy.

As she flipped through the final photos, she realized what had been the highlight of that night. It hadn't been the thought of a life with Roger Harrington. Or even the big fat family diamond he gave her. It had been the moment when she'd called her parents and they both cried over the line, telling her how excited they were to tell their friends, how wonderful it would be to plan an enormous wedding.

What she felt with Roger wasn't love. And she was fairly sure that the same went for her feelings for Brett. She was spending time mourning the loss of something that had never been there. And then Jack walked into her life and she'd told herself she still needed to heal because that was what everyone around her was saying. But did she *really* need to heal? Or did she just need to take a single step forward into her future, with the only man who'd managed to make her happy?

Her heart was saying yes, but she wanted to make sure she was thinking straight. She needed Bianca.

You up? She texted her sister a little before 7:00.

I already did my workout. Getting the kids ready for school soon.

Do you have a minute to talk?

Sure.

Lexi dialed her sister and flopped down on the sofa in her living room, staring up at the ceiling.

"What's up?" Bianca asked when she answered.

"I think I ruined my life. Again." She explained everything that had happened last night. "What do I do?"

"I can't answer that for you. Only you know what the solution is."

Lexi picked at her fingernail, thinking about how much she disliked her sister's reply. "That's not helpful."

"Fine. Let's look at the reality. I mean, a guy like Jack won't stick around forever, especially after he said I love you and you didn't respond in kind."

Her heart lurched at the thought of her panic last night. "That was definitely a mistake. I messed up."

"Well, do you? Love him?"

"Yes." As certain as Lexi was of the answer, the word nearly came out as a whisper.

"Are you sure?"

"I am. It just feels foolish. I thought I loved Brett. I thought I loved Roger. Then I thought I loved Brett again. But none of that worked out, and I don't think I can go through that again. It hurts too much to be rejected."

"And yet that's exactly what you did to Jack last night."

Lexi's stomach sank. "I know. I feel terrible."

"At the very least, he deserves an apology, right?" Bianca asked. "And maybe he's willing to talk it through with you."

"I definitely need to tell him I'm sorry. I just don't know what comes after that, and I know he's going to want to know what I think about a future."

"I want you to close your eyes," her sister told her.

"What? Why?"

"Just do it, okay?"

Lexi grumbled but did exactly what Bianca said, shutting her eyes and staring off into black and nothingness. "They're closed."

"Now imagine you've moved into your own house. Think about one of the places you've looked at. Don't think about tomorrow. I want you to think about a year from now. Imagine your furniture placed exactly the way you want it. Think about what it's going to be like on a Saturday morning, when you have the whole weekend ahead of you."

"Okay."

"What does it look like?"

Lexi imagined the house she'd liked most from the online listings. She imagined the photos she'd seen, pictured it with furniture she picked out, just for her. Everything would be perfect.

But it wasn't going to be home.

Part of that would be because it was new. But part of that would be because it would be empty. She wouldn't have anyone to laugh with. Or cuddle up with. But it was more than that. Because the only one she wanted to do those things with was Jack. He was the only person who'd made her laugh so hard she doubled over. And he was the only one with the courage to call her out when she was being ridiculous. Bianca did that for her, too, but she was her sister, and she had her own life. Lexi wanted a life for herself, as well.

"It looks sad and pathetic and terrible."

"Why does it look like that?"

"Because Jack isn't there." Lexi stifled a sob as the emotion welled up inside her. She wanted Jack. She needed him. She couldn't even envision her future without him. The only problem was that she wanted a guarantee, too. She wanted to know that this time, she wouldn't get hurt. That this time, everything would work out. It would be forever. "Oh, God, Bianca. I'm an idiot, aren't I?"

"You aren't, honey. Don't say that about yourself. You have had a very hard road to travel. Anyone would be reluctant to trust after the things that you've been through. But at some point, you're going to have to get up on that horse and try again."

"But when?" Lexi asked. "How do I know when the time is right?"

"You know what? If I were you, I'd stop focusing on the when and start thinking about the who. Jack is the right guy for you, isn't he?"

"I think so," she answered.

"Then forget the timing. You need to go to him before you lose him forever."

"Okay," Lexi said, feeling neither encouraged

nor optimistic. "I need to at least try, right? I need to make sure he knows how I feel."

"You can do it, Lex. I'm sure it feels scary, but I promise you that not doing it will feel worse. You don't want to live with the consequences of that."

"You're right. Thank you. I love you."

"See?" Bianca declared. "It's not so hard to say. I love you, too."

Lexi cracked a smile. "I need to go, okay?"

"Yes. Go."

Lexi hung up and immediately called Jack, but she got his voice mail. "Jack. It's Lexi. I'm hoping we can talk. Please call me back." She ended the call and said virtually the same thing in a text, but after ten minutes, she still didn't have a response. Her other option was to call Angie. She didn't relish the idea. Angie and Jack were incredibly close, and she could only imagine what Jack might have said to his sister after last night. But at this point, it seemed like a better choice to risk whatever Angie might say to her than to endure another minute of Jack thinking she didn't care.

"Lexi, hi," Angie said when she answered her phone.

"I need to speak to Jack, and I can't reach him on his phone and he's not replying to my texts."

"He's out on Appaloosa Island. You know how spotty the reception is out there. I texted him an hour ago and I still haven't heard back. If you want, I can tell him to call you when he checks in."

"Why is he out there? The construction is done." It occurred to Lexi that Angie was being remarkably kind to her, not treating her at all like the woman who'd stomped on her brother's heart.

"They're going through the punch list and some final inspections. Plus, honestly, I think he just likes it out there. He could've easily sent Rich to finish up."

"He does love the house." Lexi's memories of her time on Appaloosa with Jack flooded her mind. She had never felt so free as she had when they were there. Jack had opened up her whole world, which was remarkable, since they came from such dissimilar backgrounds. Logic said that Lexi was the one who came from money and sophistication, that it was her place to show him the finer things. But she knew now that it wasn't the nice things she craved. It was everything that was real. How could she have been so dumb as to have not seen that all along?

"Do you think he'll be on the site? It's massive. I could be looking forever."

"You're planning on going out there? Is everything okay?"

"You don't know that he and I broke up, do you?"

Angie audibly gasped. "I don't! He hasn't said a thing about it. But he was in an incredibly bad mood this morning. I figured he was just grumpy because the Soiree on the Bay project was done. He gets like that after a big job."

"Unfortunately, it's all my fault. I have to go talk to him. I need to explain myself before he never speaks to me again."

"Let me call Rich, and I'll find out exactly where he is. I can text it to you?"

"Sounds great. I'll leave right now."

"I'm wondering if you'll make it in time, though. He could be on his way back by the time you drive down there and take the ferry over."

"Oh, I'm not driving. I'm flying." Lexi hung up and realized that Jack was going to have to listen to her apology while she was wearing what was easily her least-cute dress and no makeup. There was no time to change into something sexier or heels, the things that gave her confidence and made her feel feminine. *Jack makes me feel like a woman.* She didn't need the trappings or clothes. She just needed Jack.

She raced to the bank, calling her dad's secretary on the way to make sure the helicopter was available. It was, and Lexi didn't even bother to stop to speak to her father, instead heading straight up to the roof and the helipad. To her great surprise, her dad was waiting for her.

"You're going to see Jack, aren't you?" Winston asked sternly.

"You can't stop me, Dad. I love him and I have to

tell him. I've been a certifiable idiot and that ends right now, okay?"

"I wasn't trying to keep you from going, Lexi." Her dad swiped off his sunglasses and looked down at her. "I only wanted to wish you good luck."

"You knew why I needed the helicopter?"

"Your sister and I talk, you know. She tells me everything. She's the one who told me I had to fix things with Jack in the first place."

Lexi should've known it was Bianca who'd set all of that in motion. Lexi would have to thank her, after she chided her for meddling. "My sister is crazy."

"She loves you. Just like your mother and I do. Just like we always will." Her dad pulled her into a hug. "I love you, Alexis. I just want you to be happy. If Jack Bowden makes you happy, I hope you'll have the courage to try to make it work with him."

Lexi smiled and sank into her father's hug. This was all she'd ever wanted from him. Ever. "Thank you, Dad. I'd better go. I don't want to miss him."

"Yes. You go on. I had Vi leave you a surprise on board." Winston shooed her toward the helicopter.

Confounded, Lexi ran over to where the pilot was waiting. He opened the door for her and she climbed inside. There was a small cooler on the seat. She buckled in, then unzipped the container. Inside was a bottle of champagne on ice and two glasses. Her dad had figured it all out. And she was so relieved.

As the rotors gained speed and the helicopter lifted into the air, Lexi looked out the window as Royal became tinier and the details less defined. That was her past, but ahead was her whole future.

It took Jack only a few hours to supervise the items on the punch list. Inspections wouldn't come until tomorrow, so he'd spend the night on Appaloosa and try to straighten out his head. Yes, this had been a bit of a fool's errand to come back to the island, but Jack needed the sea air right now. Everything in Royal felt stifling. Even out on his own property, with stretches of open land at his feet, and no one to bother him, he felt like he couldn't breathe. Life just wasn't going to be right without Lexi, and he was struggling to figure out what his next step was.

Logic said that he needed to give her space. Again. Now that he'd had a little bit of sleep and was out of the pressure cooker of that stupid cocktail party last night, he knew that he could do that. The question was how long he could keep it up. How long until he started to feel that weight again? A month? Two? He wasn't worried about meeting or falling for someone else. What worried him was that Lexi might never be ready. She'd had her heart ground into the dirt twice. That might be as much as she could take. Jack had endured it only once, and it had taken him a decade to fully recover. And honestly, he wasn't sure he had that kind of patience to wait for her to come around. He was staring down his fortieth birthday in a few weeks. It sure would be nice to know that love would be a part of his next decade on the planet. Bottom line? He wanted it all. Marriage. Commitment. Maybe even kids.

But those things seemed like an impossible wish without Lexi. Thus, he was spending his time out on Appaloosa Island, if only to clear his head.

Jack wandered over to the golf cart that belonged to the house he'd rented. He drove along, winding his way down the now-paved pathways, past everything he and his teams had built. After all the hard work they had poured into this project, he was proud of the job they'd all done here and he couldn't wait for the festival. It would be a true spectacle, a real boon for the entire area, and he was pleased that he'd had a chance to play a part in that.

When he crossed over to the western side of the island, he made his way north, up to the house he'd rented. As soon as he pulled into the driveway, his phone started buzzing like crazy with notifications.

"I must've just hit the Wi-Fi for the house," he said, pulling his phone out of his pocket. The first text was from Angie, asking where he was. Jack pinged her his location and replied that he wanted to be left alone for the rest of the day. He didn't bother with the rest of his messages. They could wait. He needed time to just be, which was exactly why he'd headed to Appaloosa in the first place.

He went inside and ran up to the bedroom to grab a clean shirt. It wasn't easy to look at that room and think about the electric nights he and Lexi had spent there. That was when he'd first known he was falling for her. Hopefully he wouldn't be stuck with nothing more than memories when it came to Lexi. It could go either way, and he had to learn to live with that inevitability.

He grabbed a beer from the fridge and headed out to the porch on the front of the house, where the long line of rocking chairs pitched forward and back in the wind. Ahead was the quiet of the private beach and the beautiful blue between Appaloosa and the Texas shore.

He closed his eyes to the rush of salty air as it blew his hair back from his face. If he had to be alone, this was the way to do it. The only trouble was he didn't want to be by himself. Life would mean so much more if he could just find the right person, or in his case, convince the right woman that he was worth the risk.

The door behind him slid open. Jack jumped out of his seat and turned. Lexi was standing there with those same island breezes blowing back her hair, looking like everything he'd ever wanted. For a moment, he wondered if he'd fallen asleep in the chair and this was all a dream. Lexi didn't say a thing. She only looked at him, expectantly. Like she wanted something but couldn't bring herself to utter the words.

"Lexi?" He took a step closer. Her sweet smell hit his nose and that was when he knew that she was real. But he truly knew he wasn't dreaming when she flung herself at him, nearly knocking him from his feet—quite a feat considering he was twice her size.

"Oh, my God, Jack. I made a huge mistake. I was such an idiot. I never should've said that I wanted to take things slow."

He gripped both of her shoulders and peered down into her stunning face. "Lexi, I don't ever want you to apologize for asking for the things you need."

She dropped her head to one side, almost as if she was disappointed. "I need you to stop making excuses for me. I messed up and I'm so sorry. I'm an idiot. Just ask my sister. She'll tell you all about it."

He shook his head. "Thank you for apologizing. I appreciate that, but I also know you didn't mean to hurt me. You were being honest, and that's not easy to do."

"But I did hurt you. It doesn't matter whether it was my intention to do so or not. It only matters that I did."

"I understand where you were coming from. I do. I had a lot more time to go through the healing process after my big breakup, and you had two to get over. I don't want you to be so hard on yourself."

"But that's the thing. If I'm not hard on myself, I'm not going to get what I want."

At the risk of repeating himself, he had to ask the same question he'd asked last night. "And what is it that you want?"

"You, Jack. I just want you."

He felt the corners of his mouth turn up in a smile, his body's instant reaction to her perfect answer. "Really?"

"Yes." She nodded eagerly. "I love you, Jack. I do. I should have had the guts to say it last night. It might sound stupid, but I think I've loved you from that moment out in front of Sheen when you said that you didn't want to talk about any man who didn't have the sense to treat me right."

"Those are just words, Lexi. Any guy can say nice things to a woman. I want you to judge me on my actions."

"And on that count, you've done everything right, too. You're always there for me. You stood up to my dad. You brought me into your life, even when you knew that I might not quite fit."

He could hardly believe what she was saying. He still wasn't sure he wasn't in the middle of a dream. "What do you want to do about this? I think you already know how I feel. I love you. I truly do. And I'm glad that you felt like you could say that to me, too, but you don't have to say something just to be with me." Cradling her face in his hands, he gently stroked her cheek. "If you aren't ready for that leap, I understand."

"I didn't say it just to hold on to you, Jack. I'm saying it because it's what's in my heart. It's what's in my head. I just had to get out of my own way. I'm ready to leap."

Jack's heart was threatening to beat right out of his chest. "What does that mean, exactly?"

She put her hand on his waist and flattened herself against his stomach. "For starters, a few days here on Appaloosa? So we can talk about what we want to do next?"

He pulled her closer and kissed the top of her head, feeling so relieved and overcome with joy that it was difficult to comprehend. He'd hoped for this moment, but he hadn't been sure it would ever happen. "You're going to have to take the lead here, beautiful. Because I want it all with you. I don't want you to buy a house. I want you to move into mine."

She pulled her head back, her bright eyes full of purpose. "We're going to have to have some negotiations about furniture. There are a few things I'd like to change in your living room."

He laughed. "Like what?"

"Do we really need a TV that big?"

"Actually, yes. We do." He leaned lower and

kissed her cheek, then her jaw. "But we can talk about furniture. I've been meaning to get a new couch."

"See? This is how negotiations go." She brought her lips to his, delivering one of her incredible kisses. It was soft and tender and everything he'd ever wanted. "I love you, Jack. I will move in with you. I will rearrange your furniture. I will do it all over again in this house if we decide to buy it. And I will stay with you as long as you'll have me."

"Forever, Lexi. That's how long."

"Forever."

Jack's smile was so wide he wasn't sure he'd ever be able to get rid of the expression. He was happier than he'd ever been. Happier than he'd ever thought possible. "Careful, Lexi. It sounds like we're making plans."

"That's exactly what we're doing. Being with you is all I want, and I don't want to wait."

* * * * *

Don't miss the next book in the
Texas Cattleman's Club: Heir Apparent series:
The Trouble With Bad Boys
by Katherine Garbera

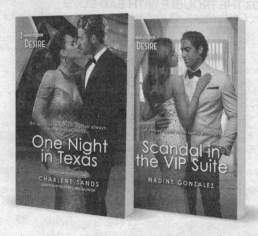

*Country music star Cash Sutherland hasn't seen
Presley Cole since he broke her heart. Now a journalist,
she's back in his life and determined to get answers he
doesn't want to give. Will their renewed passion distract
her from the truth?*

Read on for a sneak peek at
Second Chance Love Song
by Jessica Lemmon.

"Did you expect me to sleep in here with you?"

And there it was. The line that he hadn't thought to draw
but now was obvious he'd need to draw.

He eased back on the bed, shoved a pillow behind his
back and curled her into his side. Arranging the blankets
over both of them, he leaned over and kissed her wild hair,
smiling against it when he thought about the tangles she'd
have to comb out later. He hoped she thought of why they
were there when she did.

"We should talk about that, yeah?" he asked rhetorically.
He felt her stiffen in his arms. "I want you here, Pres. In this
bed. Naked in my arms. I want you on my dock, driving me
wild in that tiny pink bikini. But we should be clear about
what this is…and what it's not."

She shifted and looked up at him, her blue eyes wide and
innocent, her lips pursed gently. "What it's not."

"Yeah, honey," he continued, gentler than before. "What
it's not."

"You mean…" She licked those pink lips and rested a hand tenderly on his chest. "You mean you aren't going to marry me and make an honest woman out of me after that?"

Cash's face broadcasted myriad emotions. From what Presley could see, they ranged from regret to nervousness to confusion and finally to what she could only describe as "oh, shit." That was when she decided to let him off the hook.

Chuckling, she shoved away from him, still holding the sheet to her chest. "God, your face! I'm kidding. Cash, honestly."

He blinked, held that confused expression a few moments longer and then gave her a very unsure half smile. "I knew that."

"I'm not the girl you left at Florida State," she told him. "I grew up, too, you know. I learned how the world worked. I experienced life beyond the bubble I lived in."

She took his hand and laced their fingers together. She still cared about him, so much. After that, she cared more than before. But she also wasn't so foolish to believe that sex—even earth-shattering sex—had the power to change the past. The past was him promising to wait for her and then leaving and never looking back.

"That was really fun," she continued. "I had a great time. You looked like you had a great time. I'm looking forward to doing it again if you're up to the task."

Don't miss what happens next in…
Second Chance Love Song
by Jessica Lemmon, the second book in the
Dynasties: Beaumont Bay series!

Available May 2021 wherever
Harlequin Desire books and ebooks are sold.

Harlequin.com